GCSE History

Crime and punishment through time

Aaron Wilkes

Folens

Author's acknowledgements

The author wishes to thank Nina Randall of Folens Publishers for her hard work and patience. He would also like to acknowledge the advice and kindness of John Edwards and Lauren Richards during the preparation of this book.

© 2006 Folens Limited, on behalf of the author.

United Kingdom: Folens Publishers, Apex Business Centre, Boscombe Road, Dunstable, LU5 4RL.

Email: folens@folens.com

Ireland: Folens Publishers, Greenhills Road, Tallaght, Dublin 24.

Email: info@folens.ie

Poland: JUKA, ul. Renesansowa 38, Warsaw 01-905

Aaron Wilkes hereby asserts his moral right to be identified as the author of this work in accordance with the Copyright, Designs and Patents Act 1988.

Editor: Nina Randall

Page design and layout: Neil Sutton, Pumpkin House, Cambridge

Illustrations: Neil Sutton (pages 18, 21, 25, 48, 49, 52, 85, 87, 113 (left), Aaron Wilkes (page 32), Celia Hart.

Cover design: Richard Jervis Design

Cover image: © Hulton-Deutsch Collection/Corbis.

First published 2006 by Folens Limited.

Every effort has been made to contact copyright holders of material used in this publication. If any copyright holder has been overlooked, we should be pleased to make any necessary arrangements.

British Library Cataloguing in Publication Data. A catalogue record for this publication is available from the British Library.

ISBN 1 84303 977 X / 978 1 84303 9778

Acknowledgements

Anonimalle Chronicle: 39; AP Watt Ltd on behalf of The National Trust for Places of Historic Interest or National Beauty, 66; *BBC website*, December 2003, 122; *Chronicles of Ralph de Diceto*: 24; The *Daily Mail*, February 199[ ] 131; *Description of Elizabethan England 1577* by William Harrison, Kessing[ ] Publishing Co, 2004: 50; *Discovering the Past: Crime and Punishment Throu[ ] Time* by Ian Dawson, Hodder Murray, 1999: 75, 111; © *Guardian* Newspapers Ltd 2001, 26 June 2001, 132; *History Alive 1789–1914, Boo[ ]* by Peter Moss, Collins, 1984: 70, 75; *History V. 4* by Peter Moss, Collins Educational, 1991: 74; *In Search of History 1714–1900* by JF Aylett, Hodd[ ] Murray, 1985: 75; *Investigating History: Britain 1750–1900* by John D Clar[ ] Hodder Murray, 2003: 96; 'Justice at last, 45 years too late' by Duncan Campbell, © Guardian Newspapers Limited 1998: 139; *LCP Citizenship Resource File*, Duncan Watts, 2002, 131, 133, 133 (Q4); *Let him Dangle* b[ ] Elvis Costello. Written and composed by Elvis Costello. Published by BM[ ] Music Publishing Ltd. Used by permission. All rights reserved: 137; *Letter* [ ] *the English and French Nations* by JB le Blanc, 1737: 65; *Medieval Lives* by [ ] Jones, BBC Books, 2004: 33, 34; *MI5 website*, 123; *Past into Present 43AD–1400, Book 1*, by Christopher Culpin, Collins Educational, 1989: 3[ ] *Punch* magazine, 1851: 87; *The Anglo-Saxon Chronicle* by Anonymous, Kessinger Publishing Co, 2004: 21; *The Newgate Calendar*, 1737: 65; *The Peasants' Revolt of 1381* by RB Dobson, Palgrave Macmillan, 1983: 39; www.tudorplace.com by Edward Hall, 41.
The artwork on page 91 is based on a diagram in *History Alive 1789–191[ ] Book 3* by Peter Moss, Collins, 1984; The mind map idea is taken from P[ ] James-Pemberton: 32. Task 2 on pages 46–47 is based on J F Aylett's *In Search of History, 1066-1485*, Hodder and Stoughton, 2004.

Photos
© John Heseltine/CORBIS, 14; BBC Hulton Picture Library, 27; Mary Evar[ ] Picture Library (both), 31; ©Stapleton Collection/CORBIS, 33; The Pierpo[ ] Morgan Library, New York, 35; Robert Kett (d.1549) under the Oak of th[ ] Reformation (oil on canvas), Wale, Samuel (1721–86) / © Norwich Cas[ ] Museum and Art Gallery/The Bridgeman Art Library, 43; Mary Evans Pict[ ] Library, 45; TopFoto/Fotomas, 49; ©2005 Credit:TopFoto/Fotomas TopFoto.co.uk, 51; Mary Evans Picture Library, 58; Mary Evans Picture Library (both), 60; The Idle 'Prentice Executed at Tyburn, plate XI of 'Ind[ ] and Idleness', published 1833 (engraving), Hogarth, William (1697–176[ ] © Guildhall Library, City of London/The Bridgeman Art Library, 62; MAR[ ] EVANS/EDWIN WALLACE, 64; Mary Evans Picture Library, 66; Mary Evar[ ] Picture Library (both), 70; Mary Evans Picture Library, 71; Mary Evans Pi[ ] Library, 72; Mary Evans Picture Library (left), 74; GETTTY/TIMELIFE MANSELL (right), 74; Art Directors and Trip Photo Library, 79; National Archives, 81; National Archives, 82; National Archives, 83; Mary Evans Picture Library, 86; Mary Evans Picture Library, 87; Mary Evans Picture Library, 90; Mirrorpix, 92; Public Record Office /HIP TopFoto.co.uk, 93; MARY EVANS/DR DAVID LEWIS HODGSON (top left), 94; Mirrorpix (left) Getty Images (right), 94; MARY EVANS/DR DAVID LEWIS HODGSON, 95; Mary Evans Picture Library, 99; MARY EVANS/THOMAS PHILIP MORGAN[ ] 104; Getty Images, 105; Mary Evans Picture Library, 106; Mary Evans Pi[ ] Library, 107; Petition by Trade Unionists to the King in Copenhagen Field[ ] 21st April 1834, engraved by W.Summers, 1836, NO_DATA / © Guildha[ ] Library, City of London/The Bridgeman Art Library, 108; Royal Archives, [ ] Majesty Queen Elizabeth II, 109; Wellcome Library, London, 110; Getty Images, 111; MARY EVANS/THE WOMEN'S LIBRARY, 112; Mary Evans Pi[ ] Library, 114; NI Syndication Limited, 18/6/06, 119; P119 © POLAK MATTHEW/CORBIS SYGMA, 120–1; © Peter Macdiarmid/epa/Corbis, 123 IAN HODGSON/Reuters/Corbis, 124; © epa/Corbis, 125; MARY EVANS/ ROGER MAYNE, 127; © Bettman/CORBIS, 128 (both); David cumming: E[ ] Ubiquitous/Corbis, 129 (bottom) © MIKE FINN-KELLEY Reuters/Corbis (t[ ] © Neville Elder/CORBIS, 131; © Reuters/Corbis, 132 (top); HUMPHREYS OWEN HUMPHREYS/PA/EMPICS, 132 (bottom); Getty Images, 134; Getty Images, 135; © popperfoto.com, 137; The Idle 'Prentice Executed at Tyb[ ] plate XI of 'Industry and Idleness', published 1833 (engraving), Hogarth[ ] William (1697–1764)/© Guildhall Library, City of London/The Bridgeman Library, 144.

Some of the exam questions have been taken from the OCR (formerly M[ ] examination papers from 1988–2005.

The wording and sentence structure of some written sources have been adapted and simplified to make them accessible to all students, while faithfully preserving the sense of the original.

Contents

Crime and punishment: an introduction

The subject of crime and punishment is always in the news. Turn on your television tonight or open a newspaper and there will definitely be a report on a crime or the punishments criminals have received. The whole topic provokes massive debate and discussions run all over the country in classrooms, pubs, offices and in Parliament. But what do you think about crime and punishment? Look at the questions on this survey and make a note of your answers in your book. Try to be as honest as possible and save your answers carefully – then at the end of the course, dig them out again to see if your opinions are still the same.

Your attitudes and opinions to crime and punishment

1 Why do people commit crime?

A They are greedy

B They are poor

C They don't know right from wrong

D They are easily led by others

E Other (be specific) _____

2 Why are criminals punished?

A To teach them a lesson

B To warn others off committing crime

C To satisfy their victims

D To keep them off the streets

3 What prevents most people from committing crime?

A They know right from wrong

B They fear being caught

C They fear the consequences (court, punishment)

D Other (be specific) _____

4 **Should public, physical punishments be brought back (whipping, stocks and so on)?**

A Yes

B No

Give reasons for your opinion _____

5 **Should the police carry guns?**

A Yes

B No

C Sometimes

Give reasons for your opinion _____

6 **Should the death penalty be brought back?**

A Yes, for some crimes (be specific) _____
B No, never

Give reasons for your opinion _____

7 **In your opinion, are crime levels in the country today:**

A Worse than ever?

B About the same?

C Falling?

8 **Have you ever been a victim of crime?**

A Yes

B No

If so, were you satisfied with the way you were dealt with?

_____

9 **What do you think is the most violent period in history you will study in this book?**

A Roman times

B Anglo-Saxon times

C Middle Ages

D Tudor and Stuart times

E Industrial Revolution

F Modern times (today)

Pause for thought

Why not discuss your answers with the person sitting next to you or with the rest of the class? Why not use a computer package to present the opinions of the class as pie or bar charts? And remember to make a note of your answers.

Did the Romans conquer crime?

AIMS ....

The next four pages aim to show you about crime and punishment in ancient Rome. Aim to remember:

- how laws were made in the Roman Empire;
- who was responsible for law and order;
- how criminals were punished.

Rome was the largest and most magnificent city in the **ancient world**. At the height of the **Roman Empire**, over a million people lived there. It had many fine temples and palaces, a huge open marketplace full of shops, magnificent government buildings and several entertainment areas full of theatres, swimming baths and gymnasia. But there was a darker side to Rome too. It could be a dangerous city to walk in at night, full of pickpockets, burglars and assassins. You risked being mugged and even attacked 'for fun' by rich and very drunk young men who were looking for ways to entertain themselves. Look carefully at this cartoon based on what Rome would have looked like over 2000 years ago. Each of the eight crimes that you must look for are based on real events.

◀ **Source A** An artist's impression of Rome. See if you can spot: i) a man stealing clothes from the public baths; ii) an old man being beaten by rich youths; iii) a homeowner dumping rubbish; iv) a hired assassin waiting to kill a rich politician; v) a dishonest baker who has sold underweight bread; vi) an animal thief; vii) a murderous slave who has killed his master; viii) a line of 30 soldiers who have been beaten in battle – every tenth man has been killed. This is known as **decimation**.

What were Roman laws like?

Roman laws dealt with all sorts of crime, from the very serious (like murder) to more common crimes like fighting or theft. There were also laws to make Rome a better place to live in. It was a homeowner's job to make sure the street outside their house was clean and lighting fires in or around any of the wooden houses was banned for obvious reasons! Children learned all these laws at school and Roman rulers added new ones whenever they felt a 'crime wave' had started!

Who tackled crime?

There wasn't a police force in the early years of Rome. If you were attacked or robbed, it was up to you and your friends to catch the criminal yourselves! Then, in AD6, the Emperor Augustus introduced patrols to guard the streets and clear dark alleyways of thieves (see **Source B**). It wasn't an official police force and these men were not expected to investigate crimes, but it was certainly a direct response to the crime problem they were experiencing. However, many criminals *must* have got away with crimes because there was no official group to investigate them.

FACT *Roman laws*

The first Roman laws were written down around 450BC. They were known as the **Twelve Tables**. Over the next 1000 years, more and more laws were introduced, eventually covering every aspect of Roman life. In AD533, Emperor Justinian brought all the different laws together in one huge book called the *Digest of Roman Law*.

Could a criminal get a fair trial?

Minor crimes like theft or fighting were dealt with in a Magistrates' Court. However, you would have had to find the criminal yourself and gather all the evidence, as there wasn't a proper police force to investigate the crime for you. At court, a judge was chosen and both sides presented their evidence. The judge would then make a decision and, if necessary, decide on a punishment.

Serious crimes, like murder, were tried before a panel of judges and a jury. Again, both sides gave evidence but the jury, not the judge, decided if the suspect were guilty or not. The judge would later decide on a suitable punishment. In all cases, the accused person was declared innocent until proven guilty.

So how were criminals punished?

Punishments were used to deter others from committing crimes. As a result, some punishments handed out by Roman courts were brutal. However, how a person was punished depended on who they were (see **Source C**)!

Source B ▶
Emperor Augustus' patrols.

Up to 5000 ordinary soldiers were based in the city. Their main job was to stop riots.

7000 **vigiles** stood guard and patrolled the streets at night. They tried to stop crimes but spent more of their time putting out fires.

The Emperor himself was protected by 9000 elite Praetorian guards.

◄ **Source C** *Punishments for the different classes.*

PUNISHMENTS FOR ORDINARY ROMAN CITIZENS

You will be executed for serious crimes such as:

Treason (attacking the Emperor) or murder

Arson

Robbing temples

For less serious crimes, such as fighting, theft or dishonesty, you may be:

Whipped

Forced to pay back the cost of goods you have stolen

PUNISHMENTS FOR RICH NOBLES

You may be: Put to death for serious crimes.

But you *could* be allowed to leave the Empire for good instead. This is known as **exile**.

PUNISHMENT FOR SLAVES

All slaves in the household will be **crucified** if any attempt is made to murder their master.

FACT *Rotten Romans*

If any emperors thought the crime rate was increasing, they often responded by introducing even tougher punishments. These included chopping off arms or legs for violent crimes or pouring boiling hot metal down a criminal's throat. Anyone convicted of trying to bribe a government official, for example, would have their nose cut off before being sewn into a sack with a wild animal and thrown into a river to drown.

WISE UP WORDS

- Twelve Tables   *Digest of Roman Law*
  ancient world   Roman Empire   decimation
  vigiles   crucifixion   exile

WORK

1 Look carefully at the street scene on pages 6 and 7.

  a Make a list of all the crimes you can see taking place.

  b Use your knowledge to suggest the punishment you might expect each criminal to receive. You may want to use **Source C** to help you.

2 Write a sentence or two explaining each of the following words or phrases:

  - Roman Empire
  - Twelve Tables
  - *Digest of Roman Law*
  - vigiles.

3 a How did the Romans try to catch criminals?

  b Why were some crimes punished more harshly than others? Give an example or two in your answer.

  c Why were some groups of people punished more harshly than others?

Crimewatch

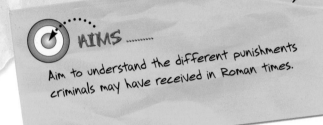

AIMS ....

Aim to understand the different punishments criminals may have received in Roman times.

We know that there were no televisions or news bulletins in Roman times. But if there had been, these two real-life murders that took place about 2000 years ago might have been presented like this. The report is based on written evidence from Roman times. As you read through the text, use your knowledge learned so far to try to work out the sort of punishment each criminal might have received.

TV presenter: Good evening viewers. Welcome to tonight's edition of *Crimewatch Rome*, the programme that brings you the latest crime news from throughout the Empire. We open our show tonight with a horrific murder … and we can speak exclusively to the victim's brother and key witness, Marcus Volusius, about exactly what happened.

Marcus: Thank you Romana. As you can appreciate, I'm still in shock but I'll try to give you as much detail as possible.

TV presenter: Take your time Marcus.

Marcus: My brother Lucius and I were eating at a friend's house and, as night fell, we decided to head for home. When we reached the marketplace, a group of drunk, rich, young men, led by Caeso, began to insult us. My brother insulted them back but Caeso just got angrier and turned on Lucius. He punched my brother to the ground and kicked him many times. Then the group turned on me.

TV presenter: Shocking Marcus. How badly were you injured?

Marcus: We were both covered in blood. Eventually, some passers-by picked us up and took us home. Sadly, though, my brother died from his injuries.

TV presenter: And what about your attackers?

Marcus: Well, you know how it works in Rome! I've got to gather the evidence myself and take it to a judge. Then he'll decide if there's to be a trial. I'm sure Caeso, a rich Roman citizen, will hire top lawyers too. We'll have to wait and see Romana.

TV presenter: Best of luck Marcus … and we at *Crimewatch Rome* hope you get over your injuries soon. Now onto our second murder, a very serious matter indeed. Over to our 'on the spot' reporter, Pliny.

Pliny: Thank you Romana. This is a murder that has shocked Rome. Macedo, a rich Roman, was having a bath when his slaves surrounded him. One hit him  in the face whilst others beat his body. They took him out of his bath and threw him on the hot stone floor to see if there was any life left in him. Some of his loyal slaves tried to revive him but the attackers ran away.

TV presenter: I understand Macedo has since died from his injuries.

Pliny: That's right Romana. And the hunt is on for those murderous slaves.

TV presenter: Thank you Pliny. Well, that's it for tonight's show. Two equally terrible murders – one committed by a group of rich noblemen; the other by slaves. But will they be punished in the same way? What do you think? We'll see you next month on *Crimewatch Rome* … and don't have nightmares – do sleep well!

FACT *What about Britain?*

The Romans spread their ideas about law and order to other parts of their Empire. When the Romans took control of Britain, they introduced their laws and their systems of policing and punishment.

FACT *Roman prisons*

The Romans did have prisons, but they weren't used as a place to punish people. Instead, they were used to hold suspects until they went on trial or their sentence of execution was carried out. People in debt were also kept in prison until they had paid off any money they owed.

WORK

1 **a** In your own words, explain what happened to Marcus and his brother, Lucius.

   b Why, according to Marcus, will he have difficulty getting Caeso punished for his crimes?

2 Design a 'wanted' poster for the murderers of Macedo. Ensure you include information about the crime, pictures and a reward. Try to include details about the motive for the crime too.

3 You may be pleased to know that the two groups of murderers were eventually caught, put on trial and found guilty. Do you think the two groups of murderers were punished in the same way? Give reasons for your answers and, if possible, try to think of the punishments the murderers may have received.

SUMMARY

- Roman laws covered every aspect of Roman life.

- The Romans established a system of policing the streets and carried out trials for minor and major crimes.

- Roman punishments were often violent and the severity of a criminal's punishment depended on their position in Roman society.

- The Romans had laws to deal with many crimes. However, we do not know which were the Roman Empire's most common crimes because there are no surviving records.

Who made the laws in Anglo-Saxon England?

AIMS

The next four pages focus on the approach to crime and punishment when the Romans left England. Try to remember:

- how the Anglo-Saxons approached crime prevention, trial and punishment;
- at least two 'ordeals' ... and why the Anglo-Saxons used them!

The ancient tribes that lived in the British Isles were known as Britons. The Romans invaded Britannia (as they called it) in AD43 and stayed for about 400 years. During that time, they ruled the Britons hard and introduced many Roman laws and customs. When the Romans left in about AD400, tribes from northern Europe called Angles, Saxons and Jutes invaded. They fought with the fiercer tribes of Britons, eventually making some of them slaves. Other Britons settled down to live side by side with the invaders. Although there seem to have been more Saxon tribesmen than Angles or Jutes, the country we now call England gradually became known as Angleland – and the people who lived there were called Anglo-Saxons. So how did they keep law and order?

During Anglo-Saxon times, England was divided into many different kingdoms, each ruled by a warrior king. Each kingdom had its own laws, made up by the ruler. At first, these laws were just remembered, but as time passed, they were written down to make them official. As you can see from **Sources A**, **B** and **C**, Anglo-Saxon laws covered every aspect of criminal behaviour – theft, violence, murder and so on – and included a system of compensation. The laws allowed a person (or their relatives) to claim a fine (known as a **wergild**) if a crime was committed against them. The level of compensation depended on the seriousness of the crime and was paid by the criminal.

Source A ▶ A few of Ethelbert's laws from around AD600. Even ten shillings was a huge amount of money for most people in Anglo-Saxon England, so the criminal often had to become a slave for the victim's family for a set period of time instead.

Selected Laws of Ethelbert, King of Kent

i) If anyone steals from a church, they are to pay the church twelve times the value of the object they have stolen.

ii) If a freeman steals from the King, he is to pay back nine times the value of the stolen item.

iii) If a man breaks into another man's house, he is to pay six shillings in compensation. The next man to follow him into the house to steal will pay three shillings; any afterwards will pay one shilling.

iv) If anyone provides a man with weapons when a quarrel has started, yet no injury results, he is to pay six shillings in compensation.

v) If a man is killed during the quarrel, the lender of the weapon is to pay 20 shillings in compensation.

vi) If anyone kills a freeman, he is to pay 100 shillings wergild. If anyone kills a rich nobleman, he is to pay 300 shillings but only 20 shillings if a slave is killed.

Source B ▾ *A few of King Alfred's laws. Alfred ruled most of southern England from 871 to AD900. As well as being a wise ruler and feared warrior, he rewrote many of the laws for his kingdom by taking rules from other kings and using them for his own.*

Selected laws of King Alfred the Great

i) Theft from a church will result in the normal fine and removal of a hand.

ii) If a pregnant woman is murdered, the killer is to pay the full wergild for the woman and half for the unborn child.

iii) If at work, a man accidentally lets a tree fall and kill another man, the dead man's family keeps the tree.

iv) If a dog bites a man to death, the dog owner is to pay six shillings. If the dog does it again, the owner is to pay 12 shillings.

Source C ▾ *Wergilds (sometimes known as blood prices) for different wounds, from laws in Kent in AD603. Some kings in Anglo-Saxon England had allowed victims of crime to hunt down criminals and punish them. However, these* **blood feuds***, as they were known, just led to more violence so the wergild compensation system was developed.*

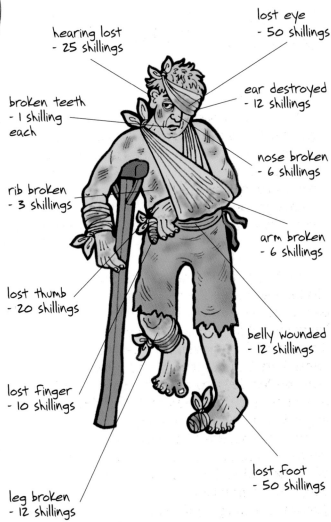

hearing lost - 25 shillings

lost eye - 50 shillings

broken teeth - 1 shilling each

ear destroyed - 12 shillings

nose broken - 6 shillings

rib broken - 3 shillings

arm broken - 6 shillings

lost thumb - 20 shillings

belly wounded - 12 shillings

lost finger - 10 shillings

lost foot - 50 shillings

leg broken - 12 shillings

Not all crimes were punished by fines. Some, like rebellion against a king or the murder of a rich nobleman, were punished with the death penalty. People who continually committed crimes were dealt with savagely. Thieves sometimes had a hand cut off or a person who told vicious lies about a neighbour could have their tongue removed!

<u>Source D</u> ▲ *This is one of the oldest surviving prisons in England. Small isn't it? Early prisons weren't used as a form of punishment. Instead, they were used to hold accused people before a trial could be arranged.*

Pause for thought

The photograph shows an early prison, used to hold people accused of a crime before trial. How are today's modern prisons used? What is their purpose? Why do we have them?

FACT *Catching criminals*

With no police force, people relied on each other to hunt down criminals. If you ever saw a person committing a crime, you had to raise the **hue and cry**. This meant you had to shout loudly and others would come to help you to hunt for the wrongdoer. People would be fined if they didn't assist. In some areas, adults over the age of 12 were grouped into ten. These **tithing**, as they were known, were responsible for each other's behaviour. If a member of the tithing broke the law, the others brought him or her to court and paid any compensation.

WISE UP WORDS

tithing   blood feud   hue and cry   wergild

WORK

1 **a** By what name did the Romans know what we now call the British Isles?

 b How did 'England' get its name?

2 Look at **Sources A** and **B**.

 a After reading each of the laws carefully, decide which laws support each of these statements.

   i)   The law was used to keep the peace.

   ii) The law was used to raise money for the King.

   iii) The law was used to create respect for the King.

   iv) Religion was very important in Anglo-Saxon England.

 b Why do you think so many crimes were punished by fines?

3 **a** Explain how criminals were hunted in Anglo-Saxon times.

 b In your opinion, do you think the Anglo-Saxon system of 'tithing' was a useful way to keep law and order? Give reasons for your answer.

 c Do you think the system of tithing would work today, in your school for example?

'You're going on trial!'

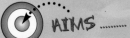

AIMS

The next four pages continue to focus on the approach to crime and punishment when the Romans left England. Try to remember:

- how the Anglo-Saxons approached crime prevention, trial and punishment;
- at least two 'ordeals' ... and why the Anglo-Saxons used them!

In today's courts, trial by jury is a common way of deciding a person's guilt or innocence. Lawyers prosecute and defend the accused person whilst a judge makes sure all the correct rules and procedures are followed. A jury of 12 men and women, who don't know the accused, then decide the outcome of the trial. Trial by jury has been common in many countries for many years. But how would you like to undergo a trial by cold water? What about trial by hot iron or trial by bread? These, and other bizarre-sounding ordeals, were common in Anglo-Saxon England. So what were these trials like? Why were they introduced? And what do they tell us about the Anglo-Saxons?

The trial

At an Anglo-Saxon trial, the victim collected all the evidence and gathered the witnesses. Towns and villages were so small that if a crime were committed, someone usually had a good idea who did it. A person could run away to live in the forest as an **outlaw** but they could then be killed on sight if found. If they went to another village nearby, they could be recognised as an 'outsider' immediately.

Trials, called **folk moots**, were held at large open-air meetings in a village. If the person accused of the crime failed to appear, they would be declared guilty. Remember, the victim collected all the evidence and gathered the witnesses.

The victim then told their version of events to a jury made up of local men who knew both the victim and the accused. The suspected criminal got to tell their side of the story too and had a chance to produce several **oath-helpers**. These were people who were prepared to swear on a cross that the suspect was innocent. In Anglo-Saxon times, few people would tell a lie on oath because they were afraid of going to hell. The more oath-helpers there were, and the higher their rank, the more reliable

they were believed to be (a priest's oath was equivalent to three peasants' oaths!). If the prisoner got enough oath-helpers (the target was usually 12), then they were allowed to go free. If the prisoner couldn't produce enough oath-helpers, then the jury used their experience and knowledge of the suspect to come to a decision. They would then tell the judge – the local lord or village elder – whether they thought the prisoner was telling the truth or not. The judge decided whether the prisoner was guilty or not and chose a suitable punishment. However, there were times when jury members couldn't agree with each other so the Anglo-Saxons developed a chilling solution ... trial by ordeal. This method of investigation took advantage of everyone's belief in God. Anglo-Saxons believed that God helped innocent people and punished the guilty. Trial by ordeal was a way of allowing God to decide on someone's guilt!

I'm innocent... but dead!

Trial by cold water

The accused person was tied up and thrown into a deep pool. The water in the pool would have been regarded as 'holy water' because a priest would have blessed it. If the suspect floated, the holy water didn't want him. Nor did God, so he must have been a bad person. He must have been guilty and would need to be punished. If the suspect sank and drowned, God must have wanted him in heaven. He must have been a good man and therefore innocent. Either way, the suspect would have died!

Trial by hot iron

The accused was made to walk three paces with a piece of red-hot iron in his hand. His hand was then bandaged and sealed by a priest. Three days later, it was uncovered. If the wound had begun to heal, the person was declared innocent because God must have thought the prisoner was worth helping. If the wound was infected, God must have thought the prisoner was not worth healing, so the suspect must have been guilty! A similar ordeal, known as 'trial by hot water', meant the prisoner had to plunge their hand into a pot of boiling water to pick up a stone or ring from the bottom instead of having to carry red-hot metal.

FACT *Where's the ordeal?*

All ordeals, except trial by cold water, took place inside a church. All the prisoners had to attend a church service on the day of their trial and weren't allowed to eat for three days beforehand.

Trial by bread

This was usually taken by priests accused of a crime. They had to pray to God not to choke them if they ate bread. Then they ate some bread that had been blessed by another priest. If they choked, they were guilty because God would not let a dishonest priest eat holy bread! Despite this ordeal seeming the least savage of all, it was actually viewed as the most effective. After all, God would never let a priest get away with a crime, would he?

The trial by ordeal system emphasises how important religion was in Anglo-Saxon times. Ordeals were 'not to be permitted except where the naked truth cannot otherwise be explored.' Indeed, as these ordeals began, a priest would say, 'If you are innocent of these charges then you shall confidently undergo this trial and the Lord, the just judge, will free you.' It seems that if human beings didn't know the truth about a person's innocence or guilt … then God definitely would!

Source A ▾ *A medieval description of a trial by ordeal. Which one does it describe?*

"It is said: 'Let this water be to thee now a trial'. The accused is undressed and cast, thumbs and toes tied together, into the water. And it is said: 'O thou water, in the name of God, do not receive this man if he be guilty, but make him swim upon thee'."

Pause for thought

This really happened in Anglo-Saxon England. A cow disappeared from a village in Wiltshire in 1012. Eadric, an old hermit who lived in the forest, was accused. Oswald, one of the Lord's workers, said he saw Eadric steal the cow. Eadric could produce only one oath-helper at the trial and was ordered to undergo trial by ordeal of hot iron. After three days, his wounds were clean and he was set free.

- Why do you think Eadric could only produce one oath-helper?

- How would we explain Eadric's clean wounds now?

- How would they have explained his innocence in Anglo-Saxon times?

WISE UP WORDS

- oath-helper trial by ordeal folk moots outlaw Manor Court Shire Court Royal Court

FACT *Which court?*

A series of courts developed during the Anglo-Saxon period. Kings would decide on some very serious cases involving leading noblemen in their own **Royal Courts**, whilst other serious crimes were tried in **Shire** (or County) **Courts** held twice a year. Here, rich lords from the area would act as judges. The most common court was the village or **Manor Court** (sometimes known as a folk moot). The local landowner was the judge and he would deal with less serious crimes, such as fighting or selling poor quality goods.

FACT *Recognise anything?*

Defendants and witnesses in court today are asked to swear an oath that they will speak the truth, the whole truth and nothing but the truth. This is something passed down to us from the Anglo-Saxon system of law and order.

WORK

1 Explain what is meant by the following words or phrases:

folk moot • oath-helper • trial by ordeal

2 **a** Name the three kinds of trial by ordeal.

b Why were these methods used?

c Would you rather undergo trial by hot iron or trial by cold water? Give reasons for your answer.

3 So what is your opinion of crime and punishment in Anglo-Saxon England? Try to summarise your findings and opinions in <u>no more</u> than 100 words:

- Were Anglo-Saxon laws harsher than you expected?
- Were they fairer and more complex than you imagined?
- Do you think the hue and cry and tithing were a good idea? What were their benefits and/or limitations?
- What about the trial system? Fair or crazy?

SUMMARY

- There was no police force to investigate crimes. People were organised into groups called tithing in which each member was responsible for the behaviour of others in the group.

- Villagers hunted for criminals themselves by 'raising the hue and cry'.

- Criminals paid compensation, known as wergild, to their victims. Very serious crimes, such as treason, carried the death penalty. Repeat offenders were dealt with savagely too.

- Trials took place in front of juries of local people. Where juries couldn't decide whether a person was guilty or not, they might order a trial by ordeal.

How nasty were the Normans?

AIMS ....

Aim to understand:

- why the Normans acted so brutally after the Norman Invasion of 1066;
- how Anglo-Saxon law and Norman law co-existed.

In 1066, Duke William of Normandy defeated the Anglo-Saxon King Harold of England at the famous Battle of Hastings. The **Normans**, as William's French-speaking men were known, spent the next five years taking all the land they could from the Anglo-Saxon English. Naturally, the English tried to fight back against the invaders but any rebellions were dealt with brutally by the Duke, who had now been crowned King William of England. Some called him 'the Conqueror'. After one rebellion in the north, William went there with his army and destroyed dozens of villages and killed many animals. Even the food was piled up and burned. Next winter, some of the survivors died of hunger – others ate the dead in order to stay alive!

Source A ▼ An account of William's treatment of northern rebels, written by a Norman monk in 1130.

" He set out to search the forests and remote mountains, stopping at nothing to hunt down the rebels hidden there. He cut down many and destroyed homes. Nowhere else had William shown such cruelty. His fury was blind and he punished the innocent with the guilty."

Source B ▼ These words were supposed to have been spoken by William the Conqueror on his deathbed. They were written down by a monk called Orderic Vitalis in 1130. Orderic was not there and was giving his own version of what William said.

" I fell on the northern shires like a hungry lion. I ordered the houses and corn with all their tools and goods to be burnt and great herds of cattle to be butchered. I took my revenge by giving them famine. Alas, I kept the throne by so many crimes."

King William was determined that people who had been beaten should stay beaten. Castles were built up and down the country to terrorise the English. He filled them with barons and knights and gave them near unlimited powers to run their regions. With no police force, it was up to these loyal followers to keep law and order. William believed that any crime was an insult to his peace so he punished people for daring to break his laws. He used the death penalty for serious crimes and fines for lesser crimes. He got rid of the old compensation system known as wergild and ordered that fines be paid to him rather than the victim. But William also kept lots of the old Anglo-Saxon laws. He was trying to show the English that, as their rightful King, he would respect their laws and customs. However, he did introduce some new laws, including the hated **Forest Laws** (see fact box).

By the time of his death in 1087, monks were writing that the crime rate was lower than at any other time in their memory. They wrote that no one dared to attack another person because they feared King William's punishments (see **Source D**).

FACT *Forest Laws*

William loved hunting deer and was determined to protect the forests they lived in. The Forest Laws banned people from cutting down trees or owning a dog or a bow and arrow if they lived near a forest. Any person convicted of stealing a deer was to have their eyes poked out!

Source C ▼ *A picture of a typical early Norman castle. These places became local centres of government, used to control the local population and administer law and order. Castles like this would later be built of stone.*

Source D ▼ *Written shortly after King William's death in a huge series of books called* The Anglo-Saxon Chronicle.

" He made the country safe. Any person could travel through his kingdom without injury, with his purse full of gold. No one dared strike another, no matter how much he was wronged … William was very tough and violent, so that no one dared to disobey him."

WISE UP WORDS

Forest Laws   Normans

WORK

1 a Who were the Normans?

b Why do you think Norman kings treated the Anglo-Saxon English so brutally?

2 a Why do you think the new Norman kings kept some of the old Anglo-Saxon laws?

b Why do you think the new Forest Laws were hated so much by the English?

Could you get justice in the Middle Ages?

AIMS ....

Make sure you know about:

- systems of crime prevention and detection in the Middle Ages;
- the development of the jury system;
- different types of punishment in the Middle Ages.

There were no policemen in the Middle Ages. If towns and villages wanted to keep law and order, they had to do it themselves. Some places set up a **watch** – a group of people who patrolled the streets each night – and a **constable** was chosen to coordinate the watch. They weren't particularly popular jobs. People didn't get paid for a start … and you lost a lot of sleep whilst walking around the streets all night. As a result, watchmen and constables didn't always do their job properly. If they did, they might be chosen again!

Villagers still tried to catch criminals they saw committing crimes by shouting loudly and getting everyone within earshot to chase the criminal. This was called 'raising the hue and cry'. Tithing were still used too, but because there was no proper police force, many criminals must have got away with all sorts of crimes. Sometimes, even the King himself got involved in murder investigations. In 1129, King Henry I fined four whole villages for not finding a murderer quickly enough!

The courts

Most crimes were dealt with in the Manor Court. This met several times a year, usually in the landowner's manor house. Here, the lord or his representative acted as judge and he would collect taxes from the villagers and sort out any arguments or problems concerning law and order. The Manor Court dealt with small crimes, such as failing to keep your dog under control or selling weak ale. A jury of 12 decided whether they thought the prisoner was guilty or not and the judge chose the punishment. Sometimes, a judge may have recommended that a crime was too serious to deal with and sent it to the County (or Shire) court, which met twice a year. This court acted in the name of the King and was sometimes known as the Royal Court. Trial by ordeal was still used up to 1215 if a jury were unsure about a person's guilt. In fact, the Normans even introduced a new kind of ordeal – trial by combat (see fact box and **Source A**).

FACT *Trial by combat*

Usually reserved for rich nobles, the two men (accused and accuser) would fight each other. The first one to surrender was declared guilty because God, the people believed, would have given the other innocent man extra strength. Over time, the law allowed a lord to hire someone to do the fighting for him. This man was called a champion.

Source A – *A medieval account of a trial by combat. Charming, isn't it? Trials by ordeal were stopped in the 1200s when the Church began to criticise them.*

" They were dressed in white leather and had wooden staves with iron heads on the ends. They had neither meat nor drink before the battle and if they needed any drink, they had to take their own piss. James lunged at Thomas, breaking his weapon. Thomas fought on until the officials disarmed them. They bit with their teeth so that the leather and their flesh were torn in many places. James grabbed Thomas by the nose with his teeth and put his thumb through his eye. Thomas called for mercy and the judge stopped the fight. Thomas admitted he had wrongly accused James and was hanged. "

One king, Henry II, made a number of key changes to the legal system in England. He decided that trials by ordeal weren't really fair so widely extended the judge and jury system. He appointed honest lawyers to tour the country and hold regular courts, hoping that these would be fairer and more consistent than some of the Manor Courts. Eventually, when trials by ordeal were finally dropped in the thirteenth century, it was trial by jury that took over as the official method of trial in any Royal Court. Despite a few minor changes, it remains this way today.

Punishments

Punishments in the Middle Ages could be brutal. Serious crimes were punished by death and frequent offenders were often mutilated. All punishments, including execution, took place in public as a warning to others. Public humiliation or 'showing' was common too. A drunk or a pair of street fighters might be sentenced to spend some time in the **stocks** or **pillory**. For small crimes though, a fine was still the most common punishment, but in some cases, a judge may have made the punishment fit the crime. For example, a fishmonger who sold bad fish might have his goods tied around his neck while he was dragged through the streets on a wooden sledge. Passers-by would be encouraged to throw rotten fruit or shout abuse at him. Thieves might have several fingers chopped off or a woman who sold bad wine could be made to drink some and have the rest poured over her head!

Source B ▾ *From the* Chronicles of Ralph de Diceto, *written in the late twelfth century.*

"King Henry believed it was his duty to prevent his subjects from running about the country robbing the poor, harming widows and orphans, raping virgins and shedding blood. Those who illegally hunted wild animals would be punished with a heavy fine or long imprisonment. Murder was to be punished by hanging; traitors were sent away to another country; those caught for less serious crimes may have their hands cut off. The King was very concerned to show fair treatment to everyone so he chose people he could trust as judges."

Source C ▾ *Crimes and their punishments. Some of these punishments may sound particularly tough, but in other European countries and Islamic civilisations they were just as harsh. Some criminals were crushed to death or stoned. Some were flayed alive, which meant having all the skin cut from your body.*

High treason (a crime against a king or country):

hanging   drawing   quartering

Murder, manslaughter, stealing anything worth a lot of money:

men hanged   women usually burned

Smaller crimes like fighting, drunkenness or small thefts:

fines   hand cut off

stocks or pillory   whipping

Source D ▾ *Examples of genuine laws and customs from the Middle Ages. Some lords enforced these laws more strictly than others.*

- All villagers to pay the same tax to the King's lord.
- All villagers to give the lord 12 eggs at Easter, or the same value in money.
- All villagers must work for the lord for a set amount of days per week. This will be changed by the lord as fits the season.
- No one can let their animals graze on the lord's land, only on common land.
- All villagers must seek the lord's permission before leaving the lord's manor.
- All villagers must seek the lord's permission before getting married.
- All barns, huts and animal pens must be kept in good repair.
- All goods sold in the village must be of a good standard.
- When a villager dies, the lord is entitled to take possession of the best animal the villager owned.

FACT *Do you know your stocks from your pillory?*

Stocks: A prisoner's feet were locked into stocks for a set period of time (for example, two days).

Pillory: Again, used for minor crimes. A prisoner's head and hands were put through holes in a wood block whilst they stood up for a few days. Often a large rock was hung round the prisoner's neck and their ears were nailed to the wood. Naughty children might be taken to a finger pillory and be trapped by just their fingertips!

FACT *Sanctuary*

If you were 'on the run', there were several ways to escape punishment. You could hide in a church and claim **sanctuary**. This meant you would be safe in the church for 40 days. If you confessed your crime after 40 days, you were made to leave the country and avoid punishment. However, you would have to carry a large wooden cross to the nearest port! Alternatively, if you could read a verse from the Bible (and not many could), you could claim **benefit of the clergy**. This meant you had the right to go on trial in a **Church Court**, usually reserved for priests. These courts imposed much lighter sentences than Manor, Shire or Royal Courts.

WISE UP WORDS

- benefit of the clergy   sanctuary   constable   watch   pillory   stocks   Church Court

WORK

1 **a** Describe how ordinary villagers helped to keep law and order.

   b Why do you think everybody was required to help keep law and order?

   c Why do you think King Henry punished four whole villages when a murderer was not found quickly enough?

2 **a** Describe trial by combat.

   b Do you think trial by combat was better than the other ordeals? Give reasons for your view.

3 Explain the differences between the following:
   - Manor Court
   - County or Shire Court
   - Church Court

4 **a** Describe the difference between the stocks and the pillory. Use a diagram to help you.

   b Why do you think so many punishments in the Middle Ages took place in public?

5 Look at **Source D**.

   a Why do you think these laws and customs were introduced?

   b Which, from the list, do you think would most annoy a villager and why?

The crazy case of Walter Blowberme

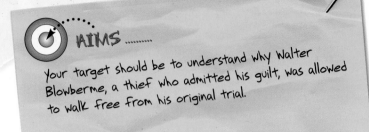

AIMS ....

Your target should be to understand why Walter Blowberme, a thief who admitted his guilt, was allowed to walk free from his original trial.

In 1249, the towns of Winchester, Salisbury and Guildford were under attack by a group of robbers. They stole clothes from washing lines, and shoes and coats from houses and shops. People in the area knew the names of the men who were responsible … but were too afraid to accuse them! Eventually, one of the robbers, a man named Walter Blowberme, was caught and he admitted his part in the robberies. Things didn't look too promising for Walter! He had stolen goods of such value that he was sure to get the death penalty. Yet, initially, Walter's life was spared! So how did he avoid execution? What happened at his trial? And what does this amazing true story tell us about law and order in the Middle Ages?

1 To save his life, Walter agreed to become an **approver**.

This meant that his life would be spared if he provided the court with the names of ten other people who were guilty of crimes.

2 Walter provided lots of names but was kept in prison until the men were found. He accused six men in Guildford of being part of his criminal gang.

All six were found guilty at trial. Walter now needed another four convictions in order to spare his life.

3 Walter accused three men in Hampshire but they were each found 'not guilty'.

Time was running out for Walter – and he still needed four more convictions!

4 Walter accused another four people of being part of his gang. One was caught but the other three ran away.

The three who fled were declared guilty. Walter now had nine convictions; only one more to go in order to spare his life.

5 The man just captured and accused was Hamo Stare. Due to the complicated nature of the case, the judge asked Hamo if he wished to undergo trial by ordeal.

Hamo chose 'trial by combat'. His opponent was to be Walter.

6 Using wooden clubs and shields, the two men fought each other.

After a fierce fight, a bloodied and battered Hamo gave in.

7 The judge declared that God must have given Walter extra strength so the Lord must be on his side. Hamo was hanged.

He's my tenth!

Walter now had ten successful convictions — six in Guildford were declared guilty, three in Hampshire fled (so were declared guilty) and now Hamo must have been guilty because God failed to help him.

8 Walter's life was spared but, at his original trial, he had admitted his guilt! As a result, he was told to leave the country.

But would that be the end of Walter's criminal career?

9 Just six months later, Walter was up to his old tricks again. He was accused of robbery in London.

This time Walter was not given the chance to become an approver. His criminal past was revealed to the judge who ordered him to hang.

<u>Source A</u> ▾ *From Hampshire Court Records of 1249. Walter is on the right; Hamo is on the left. In the background, you can see what eventually happened to Hamo.*

<u>Source B</u> ▾ *Based on the official verdict of the judge in Hampshire in 1249.*

"Walter Blowberme, an approver, accuses Hamo Stare of Winchester that they were at the house of Edeline Cross and stole clothes and other goods. Hamo had two coats as his share. Hamo comes and denies everything and says that he is willing to defend himself by his body. So there is a battle between them and Hamo gives in. So onto judgement. Because he made proof against ten men – six at Guildford, three have fled and one defended himself by his body and was found guilty – it is the verdict of the court that Walter may leave the country and go into exile."

WISE UP WORD

● approver

WORK

Pretend you write for *The Daily Blurb*, an imaginary newspaper from 1249. Your editor has asked you to cover the crazy case of Walter Blowberme. Write the news article in no more than 250 words.

You must include:

● an eye-catching headline;
● details about how Walter's life was originally spared;
● information about the trial by combat – why is it taking place, for example?
● a picture.

How murderous were the Middle Ages?

AIMS

After studying these four pages, make sure you can:
- explain the differences between courts in the Middle Ages;
- offer an opinion on whether the Middle Ages were truly violent and lawless.

Think of the Middle Ages and what images spring into your mind? Is it cold castles with dark dungeons to punish the peasants? Or callous kings and their brutal barons who owned masses of land filled with murderous outlaws? This common image of violence and lawlessness makes the world we live in seem much more peaceful by contrast. But how accurate is this view of the past? How murderous were the Middle Ages?

It is difficult to work out exactly how much crime there was in the Middle Ages. Court records like those on the next few pages are one of the best sources of information but there are problems with them. For a start, they just list crime and punishment. If you only looked at them, you would be forgiven for thinking that medieval England was packed with criminals. Court records tell us nothing about the vast majority of citizens who always followed the rules and never got into any trouble. Nothing much was ever written about these people!

Court records don't show us the real crime rate or how much crime there really was. They only show the criminals who were caught and punished. How many criminals got away with crimes? How much crime went unreported? However, court records do give us a fascinating insight into medieval law and order. Look at the following sources and come to your own conclusion on the murderous Middle Ages.

Source A ▾

Genuine County Court records

Serious crimes went on trial in the County Courts. One of the King's judges would travel to each county, perhaps twice a year, to deal with any crimes thought too serious for the local Manor Courts. Working with his jury, the judge would take about half an hour to work through the evidence, listen to witnesses and come to a verdict. These were sometimes known as the Royal Courts. The modern equivalent is the Crown Court.

CASE NO 1 Northampton 1321 – MURDER

Thomas Jordon was found dead in his house on 16 August. He had a wound on the crown of his head, which looked to have been made by a stick. It was found that the previous Sunday, a quarrel arose on the King's highway at Thenford between Thomas and John of Cornwall. John struck Thomas upon the head with a stick, inflicting a wound to the brain, of which he died. John fled but was arrested by the sheriff of Northampton. John was hanged.

CASE NO 2 London 1352 – DECEPTION

On 9 December, there was one Anthony Fowlkes, a gentleman, who deceived certain citizens. For this deception, he was judged by the Lord Mayor at the Guildhall. He was set in the pillory for two days with his ear nailed to the wood. And when he had stood for two days, he could not loosen his ear so it was slit with a knife to loosen it, and so he was had to prison for a further two days.

CASE NO 3 Northampton
1322 – OUTLAW

John of Ditchford was found guilty of robbery and murder but escaped to the church at Wootton and claimed sanctuary. He confessed to Richard Lovel and was ordered to leave the country. The court found that he did not leave the country but fled over the fields of Collingtree towards the woods. Hue and cry was raised against him and he was pursued. He was beheaded and his head was carried to the King's castle at Northampton.

CASE NO 4 Norfolk
1309 – RECEIVING STOLEN GOODS

Ellen Attehole was accused of receiving goods stolen by thieves. The jurors enquired whether anyone knew of any evil deeds done by her. People said they did not believe any of the evil rumours about her. She was acquitted.

CASE NO 5 London
1195 – THEFT

Elizabeth Hayes of Southwark broke into the house of Francis Willmore and stole two linen sheets of little value. Hayes was found guilty and was whipped at the pillory.

CASE NO 6 Norfolk
1307 – LUNACY

Andrew Friday stole the horse of John of Hales at Raveningham. It was decided by jury that he stole the horse, worth 20 shillings, on Friday and sold it to Peter Monk at Norwich market on Monday for eight shillings. But the jurors said that Andrew Friday was insane before and after the theft because of the moon. They heard that 15 days before the theft, he cut down all the trees at his home and then replanted them. When he was put in prison, he ate his clothes and the clothes of other prisoners. He was to be returned to prison to await his pardon (freedom).

FACT *What a way to die!*

Methods of execution varied from area to area. The most common way to kill a convicted prisoner was to hang them from a tree but there were other, more vicious methods of execution for criminals:

Areas of Kent – buried alive

Some coastal areas – thrown off a cliff top

Pevensey – thrown off the town bridge into the harbour

Portsmouth – burned to death

Halifax – head cut off with an axe (although execution by beheading was usually reserved for the rich)

FACT *JPs*

By the 1300s, the royal judges who visited each county twice a year couldn't hear all cases because there were so many. In 1361, King Edward III appointed important landowners and noblemen to act as judges on his behalf in their own county. He called them **Justices of the Peace**. These men took a lot of the work from the King's judges and soon became a vital part in law and order in each county.

Source B ▼

Genuine Manor Court records

Manor Courts were held regularly. Most people found guilty of offences would be fined (it was a good way for the local lord to raise money) but sometimes the guilty were humiliated by a 'showing punishment', like the pillory or stocks. Most showing punishments took place in the centre of the village as a warning to others. There are even examples in Manor Court records of villagers being executed or mutilated, but serious crimes were usually sent to the County Courts for the King's judges or JPs to deal with.

YALDING MANOR COURT: APRIL 1335

- Emma Wood for selling ale without licence – fined 1d
- Agnes Singyard for allowing her pigs to damage Cecilia Barfoot's crops – fined 4d
- John Nash for assaulting John Brickenden – not guilty
- Julia Foreman for not using the lord's oven – fined 1d
- Joanna Cheeseman for failing to protect her daughter, Elena Cheeseman (deceased) – fined 2s
- John Payne for having an unlawful relationship with Elena Clarke – whipped
- Elena Clarke for having an unlawful relationship with John Payne – whipped

STONE MANOR COURT: NOVEMBER 1335

- Nicholas Hopwood for hitting Magota, daughter of Henry – fined 2d
- Margaret Webb for breach of peace – fined 2d
- Amos Walter for theft of his lord's pigs. Also carrying a bow and arrow in his lord's wood – 2 fingers on right hand struck off; fined 2d for bow and arrow.

YALDING MANOR COURT: OCTOBER 1335

- Richard Wood for stabbing Thomas Godfrey with a knife while the two men were farming together – guilty – fled
- Margaret Mannering for not cleaning the ditch outside her home – guilty – fined 3d
- Thomas Godfrey for stealing a horse belonging to Hugh de Audley – guilty – executed
- Aymer Walter for not attending longbow practice – guilty – fined 1d
- Agnes Singyard for falsely raising hue and cry – guilty – fined 3d

FACT *How much?*

To give you an idea of how much these fines actually were, it is useful to know that in 1350, an ordinary farm worker might earn about 5d per day in summer, and 3d per day in winter.

Source C ▼ *To give you an idea of the types of crime committed in the Middle Ages, this pie chart shows the most common offences prosecuted in eight counties between 1300 and 1348.*

1 Theft (73.5%) **2** Murder (18.2%) **3** Receiving stolen goods (6.2%) **4** Arson (0.8%) **5** Counterfeiting (0.6%) **6** Rape (0.5%) **7** Treason (0.2%).

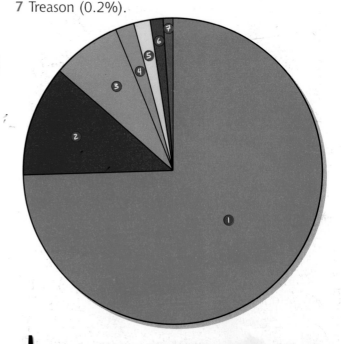

WISE UP WORD
- Justice of the Peace

Source D ▼ *This bar chart shows the breakdown of men and women accused of three crimes, based on the records of eight counties between 1300 and 1348.*

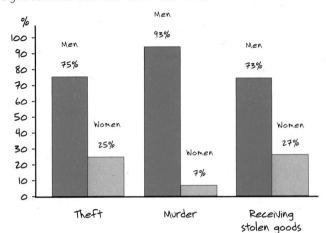

Source E ▼ *To decide whether the number of murderous crimes is great or small, the number of murders is measured against the number of people living in a certain area. This table compares London, Washington DC and Moscow from 1995 to 1997 with England in the fourteenth century.*

Place	Murders per 100 000 people
London 1995–1997	2.1
Washington DC 1995–1997	69
Moscow 1995–1997	18
England 1300–1400	12

Source F ▼ *A public whipping.*

WORK

1 Look at each of the six County Court cases on pages 28 and 29. Then copy and complete a table like the one below.

Case	Name	Crime	Verdict / sentence
1			
2			
3			
4			
5			
6			

2 Look carefully at **Source B**, the Manor Court records from Yalding and Stone.

   a What was the most common form of punishment?

   b Why do you think fines were used so often?

   c Which of the crimes before the Manor Court do you think would be referred to the County Court at a later date?

   d List three crimes from Manor Courts that are not regarded as crimes today. Try to explain why they are not crimes today.

   e List three crimes from Manor Court records that are still regarded as crimes today. Decide whether the punishments handed out in the Middle Ages were:
   i) about the same
   ii) more severe
   iii) less severe

   than what a guilty person would expect to receive today.

3 Look at **Sources C**, **D** and **E**.

   a Which three crimes were most common in the Middle Ages?

   b Write a sentence or two explaining what the chart in **Source E** tells us about the murder rate in fourteenth-century England compared to more modern murder rates.

4 So how murderous were the Middle Ages? In no more than 200 words, offer your opinion on crime and punishment:

   • In your opinion, did the courts often get their verdicts right?

   • Did the law protect England's citizens well?

   • How violent was medieval life compared to more modern times?

Source G ◄ *Two men in the stocks looking miserable. This photograph was taken in 1895, showing just how long some villages kept their stocks.*

The legend of Robin Hood

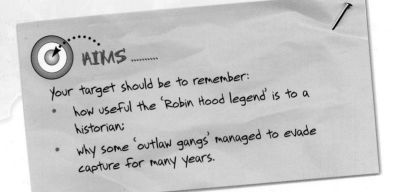

AIMS ....

Your target should be to remember:
- how useful the 'Robin Hood legend' is to a historian;
- why some 'outlaw gangs' managed to evade capture for many years.

The legend of Robin Hood is very familiar. If asked about him, most schoolchildren will instantly associate the name with Sherwood Forest, Maid Marion, the evil Sheriff of Nottingham and the idea of stealing from the rich to give to the poor. In fact, the diagram in **Source A** was produced by a Year 6 pupil when asked to 'brainstorm' what he knew about Robin Hood before starting a topic on 'myths and legends' in his primary school. But how did this legend start? Was there a real Robin Hood? And what can the legend tell us about life in the Middle Ages?

Birth of a legend

Court records from the Middle Ages mention several people called Robyn Hood or Robert Hood who were accused of crimes, not caught and declared outlaws. By the late 1300s, some manors were using the nickname 'Robin Hood' to describe any robbers and criminals for whom they had no clue as to their real identity. The term 'Robin Hood' became a catch-all expression for an anonymous bandit disguised in some way – quite literally, a 'robbing hood'.

By the 1400s, travelling storytellers told tales of a mysterious outlaw called Robin Hood who committed daring deeds and frustrated the corrupt tax collectors and cruel sheriffs. Soon, now-familiar characters appeared, such as Friar Tuck, Maid Marion and the Sheriff of Nottingham. By 1500, several Robin Hood stories had been recorded.

Source A ▶
A Robin Hood mind map, designed by Philip James-Pemberton, a Year 6 pupil from Kenilworth, Warwickshire.

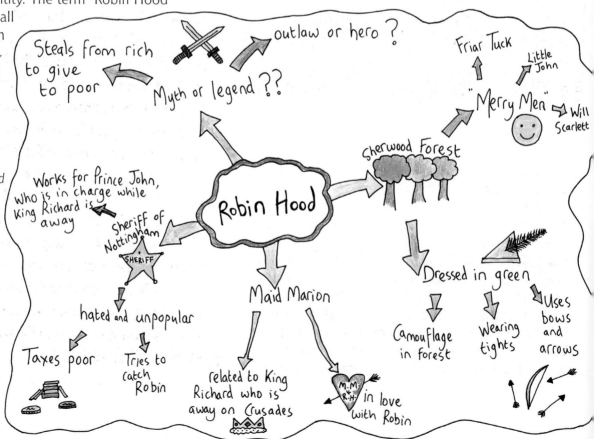

Source B ▼ *An early picture of Robin Hood.*

The real Robin Hood?

Research shows that in England's court records, there are at least eight people before 1300 who were mentioned as 'Robin Hood' or similar. Five of them were outlaws. Yet the names appear in court records in different parts of the country. For example, a Robin Hood appears in court records in York in 1226 and again in another county's records over 120 years later. It is highly unlikely it's the same man (the oldest outlaw in town?) so it seems that the term 'Robin Hood' or similar was being used as a nickname for any unknown outlaw. Irritatingly, historians will never know whether or not there was a real Robin Hood. There are certainly people accused of crimes with this name – but they certainly didn't commit the daring deeds with which he is associated.

Is the legend useful to us?

Despite the fact that we don't know whether Robin Hood was a real person, there is no doubt that his legendary story has been told for centuries. And the very fact that the story was told by generation after generation proves that Robin Hood is a very important figure – mythical or not. The legend tells us much about life in the Middle Ages. The popularity of the story shows how much ordinary people enjoyed hearing about nasty sheriffs, greedy tax collectors and corrupt princes suffering for once. The stories gave the listeners a chance to forget about their tough existence for a while and live in a world where there was plenty of food, good companionship and exciting adventures. In Robin Hood, they had a person – real or imagined – who 'put one over' on the people who ruled their lives.

Source C ▼ *From Terry Jones'* Medieval Lives.

" If there ever was a real Robin Hood, he's surprisingly hard to pin down. There is confusion over where he lived (Nottinghamshire? Yorkshire?), when he lived (the twelfth century? the fourteenth century?) and even *whether* he lived ... but the medieval landscape would not be complete without him. Robin Hood somehow represents a fundamental image of English identity – a victim of injustice and of a corrupt, self-seeking sheriff, hiding out in the forest with his company of rogues. He is a symbol of natural justice, admired by the poor and hated by the fat cats of medieval England ... In much medieval writing about outlaws, there is a presumption that their activities are honourable if robbery is performed boldly, face to face. In fact, it seems to be treated much like trial by ordeal: if God were not on the robber's side, his victim would defeat him. "

A real-life outlaw gang

Shortly after three o'clock one afternoon in July 1340, a gang of armed men broke into a church in the little village of Teigh in Rutland. The local rector, who had worshipped there for over twenty years, was dragged out into the street and beheaded. What a disturbing and horrific thing to do – even for a hard-faced criminal gang you might think! The twist, however, is that the gang of armed men who killed the clergyman weren't the outlaws – the rector was the criminal, a well-known outlaw called Richard Folville who had just started work in the church to escape his criminal past. He was one of six brothers who made up the notorious Folville Gang – an infamous band of outlaws who had rampaged around Leicestershire for twenty years.

So how did the Folville Gang operate? Why were their names remembered fondly in Leicestershire for many years after their deaths? And can they really be labelled as real-life Robin Hoods?

The Folville Gang's criminal career began in the 1320s. The six brothers, whose father was a knight and lord of a manor, first came to public attention when they joined a gang of 50 others in murdering Roger Bellars, a government official, in Leicestershire. They were declared outlaws but not caught. The brothers soon got a reputation as the kind of outlaws who righted wrongs. One monk wrote that they 'took the law into their own hands' and used force to make things right and proper. Some even used the phrase 'Folville's Laws' when they thought that a robbery or crime was justified! They killed a widely hated judge and kidnapped another who many believed to be corrupt. Local people warned them of danger when they were close to capture. In fact, the Folvilles were even paid by some to continue their life of crime and disorder. In 1331, the monks of an abbey near Leicester paid the Folvilles to destroy a watermill belonging to a rival group of monks and two years later, the King paid them, yes the King, to fight against the Scots!

So were the Folvilles the real-life Robin Hoods? Absolutely not! They committed murders, rape and robbery … and there is no evidence that they ever gave any of their ill-gotten gains to the poor (see **Source D**).

Source D ▼ *From Terry Jones' Medieval Lives.*

"The Folvilles were the younger sons of minor aristocracy, who drifted into a life of crime to support themselves in the style to which they were accustomed. They weren't robbing from the rich to give to the poor, they were simply robbing, raping, beating, kidnapping and killing as a livelihood."

The Folvilles were all eventually pardoned of their crimes after serving the King bravely whilst fighting against Scotland. The oldest brother and leader, Eustace, died peacefully in 1345. Not before, however, his younger brother, Richard, met his untimely death at the hands of a furious armed gang outside his own church. Incidentally, the men who rid the world of Richard Folville were found 'not guilty' at their trial but were forced to visit the local churches and receive a beating at each!

FACT *Get him!*

Members of criminal gangs often liked to look after one another. In Bedfordshire in 1322, one gang arrived just too late to rescue one of their members from the hangman's noose … so they killed the hangman instead!

Source E ▶ The hanging of a gang of thieves who stole from a church. Churches were easy targets for criminal gangs. At Stamford in the 1300s, a gang 'armed for war' beat up the vicar and stole items worth £10. In 1270, people complained to King Henry III that religious people couldn't pass through Nottinghamshire, Leicestershire or Derbyshire 'without being robbed'.

WORK

1 **a** Draw your own 'mind map' of the legend of Robin Hood.

   b Do <u>you</u> think there was ever a real-life Robin Hood? Give reasons for your answer.

   c Why do you think the Robin Hood legend still fascinates us today?

2 **a** In what ways were the Folville gang:
    i) similar to Robin Hood and his men?
    ii) different from Robin Hood and his men?

   b What were 'Folville's Laws'?

   c How did the Folville gang escape punishment?

Case study: How were rebels and protesters treated?

AIMS

After studying the next ten pages, you should know:

- four key rebellions and protests in the years 1300-1700;
- how the leaders of these rebellions and protests were treated ... and the reasons for their treatment.

There is a difference between a rebel and a protester. A rebel wants to change the people in charge. They revolt against a country's rulers, for example, and aim to replace their monarch with someone else. Not surprisingly, rebels have been treated very harshly throughout the years. In the later Middle Ages and Tudor and Stuart times, any failed rebels faced savage public punishments. Labelled as traitors, they were dragged through the streets to their grisly deaths in order to warn as many people as possible about the dangers of trying to remove their king.

A protester also wants change. However, they don't necessarily want to kill a king and change the person in charge; they are just objecting to the way something affects them. They want the monarch to listen to them and perhaps, if they are lucky, change one of their laws or customs.

But, whilst we can identify differences between rebellion and protest, kings and queens in the Middle Ages and Tudor and Stuart times couldn't (or didn't really try to!). As far as they were concerned, rebellion and protest were the same thing ... and were punished in the same way!

This case study invites you to study four chapters in England's history:

- The Peasants' Revolt, 1381
- The Pilgrimage of Grace, 1536
- Kett's Rebellion, 1549
- The Gunpowder Plot, 1605

For each one, you will be looking at the reasons for the protest or rebellion, the actions of the people involved and the savagery of the punishments.

Pause for thought

Ever rebelled or protested? If so, what about? What did you do? And was it rebellion or protest?

Source A ▼ *A modern historian writing about rebellion and protest.*

"Throughout the Middle Ages, rebellions by nobles were quite common, especially if a king was acting unfairly. Sometimes these rebellions led to a king being deposed. Rebellions by ordinary people were much rarer ... rebels and traitors usually faced savage deaths ... all executions were public to warn people that they must obey the King and the Church, and to frighten them away from crime. Harsh treatment of rebels who had tried to depose the King may not be very surprising. What is more surprising is that ordinary people who were simply protesting were treated in the same way!"

Source B ▾   *There are several examples of rebellion against a king or queen, usually by richer nobles and barons. Rebellions by ordinary people from the poorer classes were even rarer. The cartoon on the left depicts a group of rebels. The one on the right depicts a group of protesters.*

WORK

Copy and complete a large version of the table below.
Look carefully over the next eight pages, ensuring
you complete your chart after studying each case
study.

Name of protest/ rebellion	What did the rebels/ protesters do?	What was their punishment?	Reasons for punishment	In your opinion was it a rebellion or a protest?
The Peasants' Revolt				
The Pilgrimage of Grace				
Kett's Rebellion				
The Gunpowder Plot				

The Peasants' Revolt, 1381

One of the most famous uprisings of all, the Peasants' Revolt, is sometimes referred to quite simply as the 'Great Revolt'. But was it a rebellion or a protest? And how were the people who took part in it treated?

1 Where?

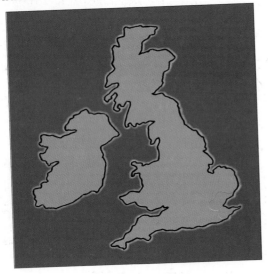

Southern England, especially Essex and Kent.

2 Who?

Wat Tyler   John Ball

Sixty thousand angry peasants armed with sticks, pitchforks, bows and arrows. Wat Tyler and a rebellious priest called John Ball led them.

3 Why?

The peasants were mainly upset at a new 5p tax introduced by King Richard II (aged 14) to pay for wars with France. Rich and poor all paid the same … so the poor hated it because they thought it was unfair.

4 What?

The peasants marched to London, causing havoc on the way. King Richard moved to the Tower of London to be safe. A group of peasants even beheaded the Archbishop of Canterbury, stuck his head on a pole and paraded it round the city!

So what happened next?

The Great Revolt only stopped when the young King agreed to meet with Wat Tyler so the rebel leader could explain what the peasants wanted. After a short meeting, the King agreed to all of the peasants' demands! However, Tyler got into an argument with one of the King's men, who drew his sword and hit him over the head. Another of the King's men pushed his sword into Tyler's belly before cutting off his head.

The young King rode out to the huge crowd of peasants and told them, 'You shall have no leader but me – I am your King!' Soon after, the peasants began to go home.

Punishment?

Despite the fact that King Richard had promised Wat Tyler that he would change things … he didn't! The King instructed his army to hunt down the ringleaders and kill them. However, just how many of the peasants were killed is still open to question (see **Sources C**, **D**, **E** and **F**).

Source C ⌄ *From the* Anonimalle Chronicle, *written by an unknown monk from Yorkshire in 1381. Much of it is based on another book written in London by a government official.*

" *Afterwards, the King sent out his messengers to capture the wrongdoers and put them to death. And many were taken and hanged at London and they set up many gallows around the City of London and in other cities and boroughs in the south. At last, the King, seeing too much blood spilt, took pity in his heart and granted them all pardon, on condition that they should never rise again.* "

Source D ⌄ *Written by John Froissart, a French knight who wrote his accounts for the enjoyment of kings and queens. He wasn't present during the King's visit to Kent and got a lot of his information from rich English noblemen.*

" *After the executions of Tyler, John Ball [and other ringleaders], the King visited many places to punish the wicked … At the village of Comprinke in Kent, all the men were assembled before the King. The King thought that not all men were equally guilty and demanded that the local leaders be pointed out. When those present heard that the innocent might escape by pointing out the guilty, they said 'My lord, here is one who excited us to rise.' The man was immediately seized and hanged: as were seven others … this was done in other parts of England where the people had rebelled so that 1500 were beheaded or hanged.* "

Source E ⌄ *From a modern history book.*

" Over the next few weeks, Royal Forces went into Essex and Kent. All the promises Richard had made were withdrawn. 'Villeins [peasants with few rights] you were and villeins you shall remain,' he told peasants at Waltham Forest. All over Essex, rebel leaders were rounded up and hanged. Then the same in Kent. John Ball was hanged and beheaded at St Albans on 15 July. His body was cut into four pieces and sent to the four ends of England. "

Source F ⌄ *Adapted from* The Peasants' Revolt of 1381, *a modern book.*

" Not many more than 100 people can actually be proved to have been sentenced to death for their part in the rising. However, the question of how many rebels were executed is difficult because at least some of the more notorious rebels were executed without trial. "

The Pilgrimage of Grace, 1536

This began as a march to London to protest about religious changes that Henry VIII had recently introduced. It ended with the pilgrimage's main leader, Robert Aske, being hanged from a church tower until he starved to death. But what was the Pilgrimage of Grace all about? What religious changes had Henry introduced? And why were Robert Aske and others punished so brutally?

1 Where?

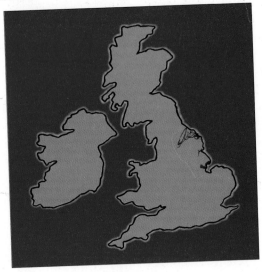

Northern England, especially Yorkshire and Lincolnshire.

3 Why?

When Catholic King Henry tried to divorce his Catholic wife, Catherine of Aragon, in 1527, he was refused ... by the Catholic Pope in Rome. Henry's solution was to change his religion. He set up the Protestant Church of England so he could divorce his wife, but this meant he had to change all the Catholic churches and monasteries too (see **Source G**). The marchers on the Pilgrimage of Grace were unhappy at the changes being made by Henry. They wanted him to change them back!

2 Who?

Thirty thousand ordinary men and women led by a one-eyed Catholic lawyer from Yorkshire named Robert Aske.

Source G ▾ *Henry VIII's orders.*

TO THE PEOPLE OF ENGLAND

KING HENRY VIII ORDERS THAT:

I)   THE CATHOLIC RELIGION IS TO BE REPLACED BY THE PROTESTANT CHURCH OF ENGLAND. SO THE KING WILL NOW BE YOUR CHURCH LEADER, NOT THE CATHOLIC POPE.

II) THE CATHOLIC LATIN BIBLE WILL BE REPLACED BY AN ENGLISH VERSION.

III) COLOURFUL CHURCHES WILL BE REPLACED BY PLAIN AND SIMPLE ONES – IDEAL FOR WORSHIPPING GOD.

IV) ALL CATHOLIC MONASTERIES WILL CLOSE (AND HENRY WILL GET THEIR MONEY!)

V)   ALL CHILDREN WILL BE CHRISTENED AS PROTESTANTS AND PEOPLE WILL BE CHARGED FOR BIRTHS, DEATHS AND MARRIAGES!

BY ORDER OF THOMAS CROMWELL
THE KING'S MAIN MAN

4 What?

They took control of Hull, York and Pontefract. In Doncaster, they stopped to talk to the King's advisors. The marchers were promised they would all receive royal pardons if they went home … and Henry would set up a special action group to look into their complaints.

Source H ⯈ *Adapted from an Internet article by Edward Hall.*

"Rebel leaders were beheaded and Robert Aske himself was carried to York to be hanged in chains until he died. Many country people were hanged in their own gardens as examples to their fellow villagers and monks of Swaley Abbey, a monastery reopened by the marchers, were hanged from the steeple of the church. In all, 216 were put to death, including lords and knights, half a dozen abbots, 38 monks and 16 parish priests."

Source I ⯈ *Henry VIII's personal orders to the Duke of Norfolk about what should happen to the leaders of the Pilgrimage of Grace, January 1537.*

"Cause such dreadful executions upon a good number of the inhabitants, hanging them on trees, quartering them, and setting up the quarters in every town, as shall be a fearful warning."

So what happened next?

The marchers took the King's promises very seriously. Despite some wanting to march on to London to force Henry to give in, Robert Aske refused to let them go, saying they were on a holy mission, not a riotous crusade! On 9 December 1536, most of the marchers went home.

Then King Henry broke his promise. Henry sent in his army to attack some of the marchers who had reopened a few of the monasteries. His men took the monks and hanged them from the steeple of their local church so everyone could see what happened to rebels. In total, over 200 of the leading marchers, including Robert Aske, were executed.

Why was King Henry so tough?

King Henry only kept his promises when it suited him. People who knew him well knew that this love could turn to hate very quickly. As far as Henry was concerned, any protest against a decision he had made was a personal insult. And at a time when kings believed they were chosen by God to lead their country, an argument with a king would be the same as arguing with God and no one would think of doing that. In Henry's mind, he had to be tough on any protesters in order to maintain the natural, God-given order of things.

Henry also felt he had to be tough to show other countries that he was in control. He had annoyed most of Catholic Europe by changing religions – a protest in England might just be the chance another country needed to invade, get rid of Henry and return Catholicism to England.

Kett's Rebellion, 1549

In 1549, the people of Norfolk had two major problems – there were too many sheep … and not enough jobs. Complaints grew into a major protest, which ended up in a huge battle that saw 3000 protesters killed.

1 Where?

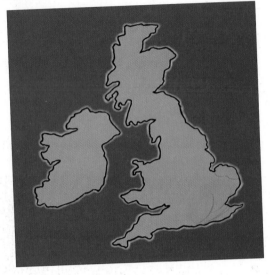

In and around the county of Norfolk.

2 Who?

Robert Kett

A mix of townspeople, farmers and ordinary workers. A local Norfolk landowner named Robert Kett led them.

3 Why?

Sorry lads, we only need a couple of you. These little beauties don't need much looking after.

Fortunes were being made from the wool trade. Many landowners in Norfolk (and other places) had enclosed their farmland – they had fenced it off to graze more and more sheep. This was disastrous for farm labourers because sheep farming employed fewer people than crop farming.

4 What?

ENCLOSE OUR LAND WOULD YOU?

MY FAMILY HAS BEEN GROWING CROPS HERE FOR CENTURIES

NORWICH

In July 1549, a large group of protesters began ripping down fences near Norwich. Sixteen thousand of them, led by Robert Kett, then moved towards the city and camped outside its walls. They sent a list of 29 complaints to Edward VI, the new nine-year-old King, mainly to do with their poor standard of living. The King sent a messenger to tell them they would all receive royal pardons if they went home … but he was told by one young protester to 'kiss his backside' (see **Source J**).

So what happened next?

By August, the protesters had received no more messengers from the King. They entered Norwich, took over and tried to capture Yarmouth. The King sent in the Earl of Warwick and an army of 10 000 men to deal with them. Three thousand rebels were killed in the battle that followed.

Punishment?

Robert Kett was taken to Norwich Castle as a traitor and hung by chains over the castle walls until he died. His body remained there for nearly a year, until the smell got too bad and it was removed.

Source J ▾ *This eighteenth-century painting shows Robert Kett refusing the offer of a king's pardon. Note the rude (and quite funny) response of one young protester (dressed in green).*

Up to 300 others were executed in total, most of them hung up around Norwich. Nine of the more senior leaders were hung, drawn and quartered near to a tree on top of a hill near Norwich where the leaders had held meetings.

Source K ▾ *Kett's sentence, which wasn't actually carried out. He was starved to death and hanged in chains instead! A 'better' punishment or not?*

"Kett be dragged to Tyburn, where he is to be hung and whilst still alive his entrails [insides] taken out and burned before him, his head cut off and his body cut into four pieces."

The Gunpowder Plot, 1605

In January 1606, eight plotters (including Guy Fawkes) were cruelly and publicly punished for high treason – a crime against a monarch or country. So what exactly had these plotters planned? How closely did they come to killing their King? And why, after over 400 years, do we still remember the gunpowder plotters of 1605?

1 Where?

London.

3 Why?

How dare he fine us?

We should kill him.

We could replace him with his daughter and bring her up as a Catholic.

James I had been King for two years. Many English saw him as rude and ill mannered – and he was a foreigner from Scotland. In a time of continued religious conflict between Protestants and Catholics, the new Protestant King ordered that Catholics who didn't attend Church of England services should be fined. He even declared that he 'detested the superstitious Catholic religion'!

2 Who?

Thomas Percy   Chris Wright   John Wright   Guido (Guy) Fawkes   Robert Winter   Robert Catesby   Thomas Winter

A group of fanatical, Catholic gentlemen from established families, led by the charismatic Robert Catesby. He was brave and handsome, but a liar and a gambler.

4 What?

The plotters hired a cellar under Parliament. They were going to blow up James when he opened Parliament on 5 November. Thirty-six barrels of gunpowder were put in place and primed to explode.

So what happened next?

A few weeks before 5 November, a letter had arrived at the home of Lord Monteagle, the brother-in-law of one of the plotters, warning of a 'terrible blow' that was due to happen when Parliament opened. Monteagle went to the King, who sent instructions to arrest the plotters just before the opening in order to arrest the culprits 'red-handed'.

Twelve hours before the King was due to meet Parliament, the cellars were searched. Fawkes, using the false name of John Johnson, was found and arrested. Under torture (on the rack), he eventually gave his real name and details of the plot. Soon, the enemy plotters were found; four were shot and the rest taken to London for trial.

The full story?

Much of what we know about the Gunpowder Plot is the official government story written by Robert Cecil, the King's chief minister. For centuries, historians have wondered whether Cecil told the whole truth. For example, why were a group of known Catholics allowed to rent a cellar under Parliament? How did the plotters get so much gunpowder when the government strictly controlled it? Why was the man suspected of writing the warning letter to Lord Monteagle – a plotter named Francis Tresham – not arrested with the other plotters (he later died of a 'mystery' illness)?

There is little doubt that there was a Catholic plot to kill King James. But how much the government knew about it, even encouraged it, is still open to debate! After all, when news of the plot reached ordinary people, there were celebrations to mark the safekeeping of their King. It seems that the failed plot had made an unpopular King more popular than ever before!

Punishment?

Source L shows the fate of the remaining plotters. Having confessed under torture, they faced a quick trial and were found guilty. In January 1606, they were dragged through London's streets, hanged (but taken down alive), castrated, cut open, beheaded and cut into pieces. Different body parts were sent to different areas of the country as a warning to others. Their heads were stuck on spikes on top of the Tower of London and London Bridge.

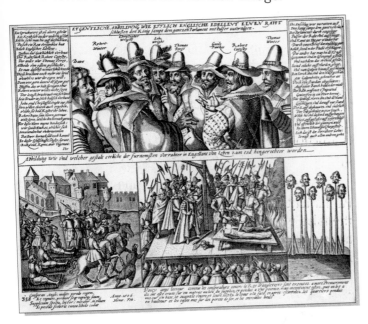

FACT *Clever Guy*

Guy Fawkes himself was probably dead before his punishment properly began. As he climbed up the steps towards the hangman's noose, he jumped off the scaffold, head first, and broke his neck. The execution carried on regardless.

Source M ▾ *The words of the judge announcing the plotters' sentence.*

"The traitor is to be drawn backward behind a horse to the place of execution from his prison, as he is not worthy to tread upon the face of the earth … he will then be hanged up by the neck between heaven and hell as he is not fit to breathe the common air … then he is to be cut down alive and have his private parts cut off and burned before his face for he is unfit to leave any children after him. His bowels, heart and other parts will be taken out and burned. After his head, which imagined such evil, has been cut off, his body is to be quartered and set up in a high place to be viewed."

SUMMARY

* Punishments were harsh and took place in public to frighten others away from a life of crime.

* Laws dealt with all types of crime. The lord of the manor laid down local laws.

* Trial by jury was used for most offences after trial by ordeal ended in the thirteenth century. Royal judges toured the country to see serious cases. Justices of the Peace held County Courts and each manor had their own court too, run by the local lord.

Source L ◂ *An engraving by Hoogenborgh, 1605.*

Have you been learning?

TASK 1: HUNT THE LEGEND

Draw this puzzle in your book and fill in the answers to the clues. A name will reveal itself in the middle (clue 10). Write a sentence or two about this person.

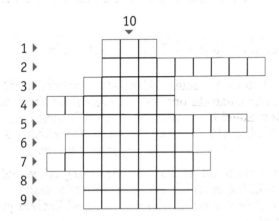

1 Hue and _____

2 In charge of the watch

3 To revolt

4 An Anglo-Saxon fine

5 Hiding in a church meant you were claiming this

6 Responsible for each other

7 5 November plot

8 Not a pillory

9 Hot iron, cold water, combat or bread!

TASK 2: LIFE AIN'T PLEASANT FOR A PEASANT!

One of the most famous rebellions in English history is the Peasants' Revolt. Here are two accounts of what happened on 15 June 1381. Read them carefully and answer the questions that follow:

Source A Written by Sir John Froissant, who was not present at the event he describes.

'Wat Tyler spurred his horse and came close to the King. Then he said, "Do you think, King, that these people will go away from you without having your signed guarantees?" "No," said the King, "you shall have them. They are ordered for you and shall be given to everyone. So, good fellows, go back to your people and get them to leave London."

Wat Tyler cast his eyes on a squire who was there carrying the King's sword. Wat Tyler hated that squire because he had annoyed him before. "Give me that sword," said Tyler. "No," said the squire. "It is the King's sword. You are not fit to have it, for you are only a knave." "By my faith," said Tyler, "I shall never eat meat until I have your head."

At that moment the Mayor of London arrived with twelve knights, all well armed, and broke through the crowd. He said to Tyler, "Ha! Would you dare to speak like that in front of the King?" The King began to get angry and told the Mayor, "Set hands on him." Tyler said to the Mayor, "What have I said to annoy you?" "You lying, stinking crook," said the Mayor, "would you speak like that in front of the King? By my life, you'll pay dearly for it."

And the Mayor drew out his sword and struck Tyler such a blow on the head that he fell down at the feet of his horse. The knights clustered round him so he could not be seen by the rebels. Then a squire called John Standish drew out his sword and put it into Tyler's belly and so he died.

Seeing their leader killed, the people began to murmur and said, "Let us go and kill them all." And they got themselves ready for battle.

The King rode alone to these people and said, "Sirs, what is the matter? You shall have no leader except me. I am your King. Be peaceful."

Most of the people were ashamed and began to leave.'

Source B An account from the City of London Record Book.

Wat Tyler   John Ball

'In front of the King, with the lords and knights on one side and the angry mob on the other, Sir William Walworthe bravely rushed upon Walter Tyler while he was arguing with the King and the nobles. He first wounded him in the neck with his sword, then threw him from his horse, fatally wounding him in the chest.

Then he rode on with the King. Meanwhile, the whole of the angry mob was getting ready against the King and refusing to make peace unless they first had the head of the Mayor.

The Mayor himself went into the City at the request of the King. In half an hour, he led a great force of Londoners to help the King. The whole crowd of madmen was surrounded. Not one of them would have escaped if the King had not advised them to go away.

So the King returned to the City with the greatest of glory, and all the wicked crowd fled at once to hide.

The King himself knighted the Mayor for what he had done.'

1 Having read **Source A**, what new evidence do you get from **Source B**?

2 **a** Make a list of differences between the two pieces of evidence.

   b Can you explain why these differences occur?

3 Do you think the writer of **Source B** supports the peasants or not? Write down words or phrases that show whether he does or doesn't support them.

TASK 3: SUMMARY

Draw a table like the one below into your book. Using your knowledge of crime and punishment in the Roman Empire and Medieval England, try to fill in your table. The first box has been started for you.

	ROMAN EMPIRE	MEDIEVAL ENGLAND	IN YOUR OPINION, DID THINGS CHANGE OR STAY THE SAME?
LAWS	They were made by the Emperor and the ruling body. They were written down and covered most types of crimes.	Laws were made by the King and his local lords and barons. They covered all sorts of crime.	
POLICING			
TRIALS			
PUNISHMENTS			

TASK 4: QUESTION TIME

Look at these genuine GCSE questions carefully. Why not try to complete one, two or even all of them as a revision exercise? In brackets after each question, you will find the pages of this book where there is information that might refresh your memory.

- How much did methods of preventing crime and punishing criminals change from early Saxon times to the end of the Middle Ages? Explain your answer.
  (pages 12–45)

- During the medieval period, the English system of law and order gradually developed. Briefly explain the main features of the Anglo-Saxon system of justice.
  (pages 12–17)

- To what extent did the Normans make changes to the system of law and order in England? Explain your answer.
  (pages 20–45)

- How successful was the medieval system of law and order? Explain your answer.
  (pages 12–45)

'In terror of the tramp'

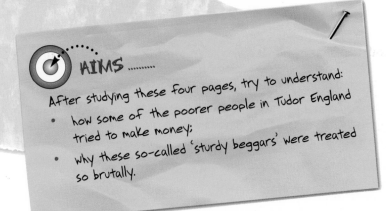

AIMS

After studying these four pages, try to understand:
- how some of the poorer people in Tudor England tried to make money;
- why these so-called 'sturdy beggars' were treated so brutally.

In Tudor England, one of the most infamous types of criminal was the **sturdy beggar**. These were tramps and vagrants who wandered around the country either looking for work … or looking for goods to steal or people to trick so they didn't have to work at all. One writer reckoned there were over 10 000 of them out of a population of around five million. Gangs of sturdy beggars roamed England looking for 'victims' to rob or trick. In fact, many people at the time described themselves as 'living in terror of the tramp'! So how exactly did sturdy beggars operate? What con tricks did they try? Why did the number of sturdy beggars suddenly increase in Tudor England? And how were they punished if caught?

The origin of the sturdy beggar

The number of poor people increased in Tudor England. The first Tudor King, Henry VII, banned his rich barons from keeping private armies so lots of men lost their jobs as soldiers. To make matters worse, many large landowners started to keep sheep on their land rather than allow tenants to hire it and grow crops. This meant fewer jobs as tenant farmers and their workers and families had to leave their manors to fend for themselves. Later, when Henry VIII closed all the monasteries, the increasing number of poor people couldn't even go to the local monks for their handouts.

All this led to an increase in the number of poor people wandering the streets looking for food and shelter. These **vagabonds**, as the Tudors called them, were a mixture of unemployed soldiers and farmers, women and children, the old and sick. A small minority, who were fit enough to look for work, found that crime was an easier way for them to make a living. In Tudor England, this rough, tough, devious bunch of vagabond con men were also known as 'sturdy beggars'.

Types of sturdy beggar

In 1567, a man named Thomas Harman wrote a best-selling book warning against the dangers of sturdy beggars. He described 23 different types of these tricksters, some of whom are detailed here.

The Bristler

The Bristler would use specially weighted dice ('bristles' were loaded or crooked dice), which would land on whichever number the Bristler chose.

The Counterfeit Crank

Dressed in old, grubby clothes, he would pretend to have violent fits. He would often suck soap so that he frothed at the mouth! The worse he shook, the more money he hoped to attract because people would feel sorry for him.

The Clapper Dudgeon

He would cut his skin to make it bleed and tie dirty rags over the wounds to make it look even worse. He hoped people would feel sorry for him and give him money so he could get medical attention.

The Baretop Trickster

She would flash at a man in the street and ask him to buy her a meal. The man, thinking he might get to have sex with the woman, would accompany her to a nearby house … where a vicious gang would be waiting to rob him!

Tom O'Bedlam

He would pretend to be mad and follow people around. Often he would carry a stick with a piece of meat attached to the end or spend hours barking like a dog or stuffing chicken heads into his ears. Why do you think people gave him money?

Source A ▾ *A picture of Baretop Tricksters that appeared in a warning leaflet in the 1500s.*

Source B ▾ *Some other sturdy beggars, as featured in Harman's 1567 book about them.*

The Cutpurse — a pickpocket who would secretly creep up behind you, cut a hole in your pocket or bag and steal the contents.

The Angler — fixed a hook to a long stick and stole clothes from washing lines.

The Dummerer — pretended to be deaf and dumb, hoping people would feel sorry for him.

Priggers of Prancers — horse thieves.

Rufflers — ex-soldiers who beat people up to get their purses.

FACT *What did he say?*

Sturdy beggars developed their own language, a kind of slang known as **canting**. They used it to speak secretly to other thieves on busy streets. Amazingly, some 'canting' words managed to work their way into everyday use. For example, booze (meaning 'alcohol'), peck (meaning 'food' – ever said you were 'peckish'?), duds (meaning 'clothes'), lift (meaning 'steal') and beak (meaning 'police' or the 'law') will still be recognisable to some of you today!

As the number of sturdy beggars increased, they became one of the ruling classes' biggest headaches. They were thought to be behind all sorts of crime and, in 1531, the government took firm action.

Whilst some old and sick people were given a special licence to beg, those who weren't given one would be whipped until their 'bodies be bloody' if they were caught out on the streets. If they were caught again, they had a 2½cm hole bored through the ear, whilst a third conviction meant death by hanging! At one point, during Edward VI's reign, any person found begging even ONCE would be made a slave for two years and branded on the forehead with the letter V (for vagabond)!

Source C ▾ *From William Harrison's* Description of England, *published in 1577.*

"The vagabond abide nowhere but runneth up and down from place to place. Idle beggars make corrosives and apply them to the fleshy parts of their bodies ... to raise pitiful sores and move the hearts of passers-by so they will bestow large gifts upon them. How liberally they beg, what forcible speech that makes me think that punishment is more suitable for them than generosity or gifts.

They are all thieves and extortionists. They lick the sweat from the true labourers' brows and take from the godly poor what is due to them. It is not yet 60 years since this trade began but how it has prospered since that time is easy to judge for they are now supposed to amount to 10 000... Moreover, they have devised a language among themselves which they name canting such as none but themselves are able to understand."

Source D ▾ *From Middlesex County Records, 1573.*

"29 March 1573. At Harrow on the Hill in Middlesex, on the said day, John Allan, Elizabeth Turner, Humphrey Foxe, Henry Bower and Agnes Fort, being over 14 years and having no lawful means of livelihood, were declared vagabonds. Sentenced to be flogged and burned through the right ear."

Gradually, it became clear that most vagabonds were not a threat to law and order at all. Instead, they were just genuinely poor and unemployed people who were looking for work. In the late 1500s, various laws were passed that ordered each district or parish to provide money for the poor. Queen Elizabeth I went one step further in 1601 when she backed the first official Poor Law. This said that each area should tax wealthy local people and use the money to provide work and support for the old and sick. The law still maintained that anyone who refused to work should be whipped and then put in a **House of Correction**. There, they had to make things that were later sold. Even their children were taken from them and given jobs. Not surprisingly, some beggars were so afraid of the House of Correction that some cities reported a drop of 90% in the number of people wandering the streets!

Source E ▾ *How the Tudors treated sturdy beggars.*

Date of law	King or Queen	Action
1495	Henry VII	Beggars to go in stocks for three days, then sent back to their birth-place or previous residence.
1531	Henry VIII	Some 'worthy' poor, old and sick given licence to beg. Others should be whipped and sent back to where they came from. Harsher punishments for repeat offenders.
1547	Edward VI	Beggars whipped and branded with a V on forehead (for vagabond). Also to be made a slave for two years. If they offend again or try to escape, they will be executed (this law remained in force for three years before it was changed back to the 1531 law because it was viewed as too severe).
1601	Elizabeth I	Local taxes should help the poor. Poor people who refuse to work should be imprisoned. Beggars will still be whipped until they bleed and sent back to where they came from.

Source F ▾ *A beggar being whipped through the streets in 1577.*

WISE UP WORDS

- sturdy beggar   vagabond
  House of Correction   canting

WORK

1 **a** Why did the number of poor people increase in Tudor England?

   b What was a 'sturdy beggar'?

2 **a** Write down three examples of how sturdy beggars were punished if caught.

   b Why do you think Tudor kings and queens treated sturdy beggars so brutally?

3 Look at **Source E**. In what ways did the Poor Law of 1601 differ from earlier laws that dealt with poorer people?

4 **a** Here are five ways of punishing sturdy beggars – whipping, branding, hanging, put in a House of Correction, made into a slave. Write down the one you think was the most suitable punishment and explain why you chose it.

   b Why don't <u>you</u> think we punish poor people and beggars today?

5 The year is 1543 and you work as a printer in a large town. The Mayor has asked you to design a leaflet warning visitors about the dangers of sturdy beggars. Your warning leaflet should include details about some (or all) of the sturdy beggars mentioned on these pages and about how they might try to trick someone. Remember: It is a warning leaflet, so it needs to be bright, colourful and easy to read.

What did the Scottish Boot, the Juda Cradle and the Spanish Donkey have in common?

AIMS ....

Aim to understand why and how torture was used in England during this time.

In Tudor and Stuart England, crimes were punished in much the same way as they had been in the Middle Ages. The stocks and pillory were still used regularly but fining a criminal was still the most common way of punishing minor crimes. For serious offences, there were still very harsh punishments. In 1533, a cook was boiled to death in a cauldron for trying to poison the Bishop of Rochester (judges were perhaps trying to make the punishment fit the crime!).

Some towns still had watchmen and constables to look out for crooks, and Justices of the Peace tried to investigate crimes, gather information and hold trials. However, these government-appointed men were also busy with other duties, such as looking after roads and bridges, checking alehouses and reporting people who continually failed to attend church! As a result, the government sometimes used other ways of getting information, catching criminals and foiling plots. One way was to employ spies but this was time-consuming and costly (you had to pay the spy of course). A much more brutal solution was to use torture!

The Rack

How did it work?
A prisoner was stretched for hours on end. Often, their tendons and ligaments would tear and their shoulders would become dislocated.
Fact: There was only one rack in the whole of England, which was kept in the Tower of London. One famous Tudor rack torturer boasted that most of his victims were a foot longer by the time he had finished with them.

The Press

How did it work?
A prisoner would lay under strong wooden or metal boards whilst heavy stones were placed upon them. If a prisoner failed to own up to their crimes, another heavy rock could be placed on them.
Fact: One press operator once boasted that he knew his victim would not be able to hold out much longer 'as soon as I heard his chest crack'.

The Spanish Donkey

How did it work?
Weights were attached to a prisoner's legs whilst they sat astride the wooden 'donkey'. More weights were applied until the prisoner confessed.
Fact: A torture first used in Spain, the idea was to destroy a victim's genitals!

The Juda Cradle

How did it work?

A victim was hung above a cone pyramid and then lowered onto it. The sharp tip of the cone was forced up into the area between the prisoner's legs.

Fact: Visitors are told about this torture on a tour of the Tower of London; it usually gets the biggest gasps!

The Scottish Boot

How did it work?

A prisoner's foot was placed in a heavy metal boot and wooden wedges would be hammered down the sides. Gradually, the leg and anklebones would be crushed and splintered into pieces.

Fact: A similar contraption called the Copper Boot was sometimes used. For this torture, molten red-hot lead was poured into a boot, giving the victim terrible burns.

Skeffington's Irons

How did it work?

Specially designed to keep the prisoner in a very uncomfortable position. Either they owned up to the crime ... or their back was broken.

Fact: This torture was named after its inventor, Leonard Skeffington, who was once head torturer for Henry VIII.

Source A ▾ *Father Gerard, a Catholic priest, was tortured in the Tower of London in 1597.*

" ...Then they took me to a big upright pillar. Driven into the top of it were iron staples for supporting heavy weights. They then put my wrists in iron gauntlets [gloves] and ordered me to climb some wooden steps.

My arms were lifted up and an iron bar was passed through the rings of one gauntlet, then through the staple and the rings of the second gauntlet. They fastened the bar with a pin. Removing the steps, they left me hanging with my hands and arms fastened above my head. The tips of my toes, however, still touched the ground and they had to dig away at the earth from under them.

I began to pray. The gentlemen asked me whether I was willing to confess now. "

WORK

1 **a** What were the two main methods used to get information in Tudor England?

   b Why did the Tudors favour torture over the use of spies?

   c List as many reasons as you can why we don't torture suspected criminals today.

2 Look at **Source A**.

   a In your own words, describe how Father Gerard is being tortured.

   b Why did earth have to be dug away from under the prisoner's feet?

3 Most of this torture equipment still survives today, kept on display in the Tower of London. Design an information leaflet for a young schoolchild to use as a guide on a torture chamber tour. Include:
   * Colourful pictures of the torture instruments
   * Facts about how they worked
   * A background to torture
   * An imaginative title, for example, 'The Tower's Terrible Torture Guide'.

Why was Christmas banned?

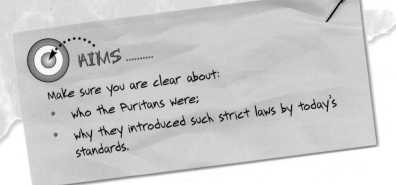

AIMS ....

Make sure you are clear about:
- Who the Puritans were;
- Why they introduced such strict laws by today's standards.

There have been times in England's history when some of the things we enjoy and take for granted today have been banned. For example, Edward III banned football for a while in 1314 because he wanted people to devote more time to practising their archery skills in case England were invaded. Queen Elizabeth even introduced a law forcing people to wear more woollen clothing so she could make even more money by taxing England's world-beating wool industry! However, some of the laws introduced by the Puritan government in the 1640s and 1650s take some beating! This was a time when going for a walk or having your hair cut on a Sunday, visiting a theatre or swearing, became crimes. And yes, even Christmas Day was banned in 1652!

So why were these laws introduced? Who were the Puritans that introduced them? And why, of all things, did they decide to turn celebrating Christmas into a crime?

Who were the Puritans?

The Puritans were a Christian group who read the Bible closely. It taught them how Jesus had led a simple life – eating simple food and wearing plain clothes. Puritans thought all people should do the same so chose to wear dull, plain clothing instead of the bright, fashionable clothing of the day. They believed passionately that Sundays should be a day of rest, for worship only, and wanted to control people's behaviour in order to save them from hell. After the death of Elizabeth I in 1603, the Puritan way of life increased in popularity. And by the 1640s and 1650s, they controlled Parliament ... so were free to introduce many new laws!

Source A ▶ How the Puritans dressed.

New laws

The Puritans introduced laws in order to force people to follow their strict Puritan lifestyle. They believed that you had to work hard if you wanted to go to heaven when you died so they banned anything that interfered with work or worship. As a result, many inns and taverns were shut and all theatres were closed. Most sports and games were banned on Sundays and any activity involving gambling (horse-racing, cock-fighting and bear-baiting) was outlawed altogether.

Source B ▾ *How the Puritans dealt with lawbreakers.*

3

OFFENCE: mending a dress on a Sunday

PUNISHMENT: put in stocks for three days

1

OFFENCE: playing football on a Sunday

PUNISHMENT: whipped

4

I wish they'd stop %*!X fining us for *%!X*% swearing.

OFFENCE: swearing

PUNISHMENT: fine, but if you continued to swear, you would go to prison

2

OFFENCE: getting hair cut or beard trimmed on a Sunday

PUNISHMENT: fine

5

OFFENCE: walking to the next village on a Sunday

PUNISHMENT: fine

Source C ▾ *A typical act of the strict Puritan government. A new fine system was introduced to combat swearing, and adultery was made an offence, punishable by death.*

Whoever shall be guilty of the offences mentioned here on the Lord's Day and they be of the age 14 and upwards shall, for every offence, pay ten shillings, [about 50p today]:

- *using any boat, ferry, barge, horse or coach – except that it be to and from some place for the service of God;*

- *being in any tavern, tobacco house, shop or sending for any wine, ale, beer or tobacco;*

- *dancing or singing or playing musical instruments;*

- *selling goods on the Lord's Day;*

- *walking for no reason.*

Source D ▾ *A popular poem written by Richard Braithwaite in 1638. Note that he wrote it some time <u>before</u> the Puritans dominated the government.*

> *"One day to Banbury I came,*
>
> *And there I saw a Puritan,*
>
> *Hanging up his cat on Monday,*
>
> *'Cos it killed a mouse on Sunday."*

So why was Christmas banned?

Take this down

Christmas Day itself was abolished in 1652. It was also made illegal to celebrate Easter or Whitsun. They were banned because the Puritans believed that they were not true Christian festivals. They argued that they were ancient pagan festivals from before the time of Christ, which had been adopted by the Christian Church. They abolished them because they thought people would go to hell for celebrating a non-Christian festival. In their place, a new holiday was introduced on the second Tuesday of every month … but eating was banned on these days!

So singing carols, putting up decorations of holly and eating plum pudding and mince pies on 25 December were crimes in Puritan England. On one occasion, soldiers even went round houses in London and confiscated all the meat for Christmas dinner.

Why were the laws repealed?

By 1658, Puritan rule was becoming more and more unpopular. Many ordinary people just didn't want to live by these strict laws any more. In September of that year, Oliver Cromwell, one of the leading Puritans and Lord Protector of England, died of malaria. His Puritan son, Richard, took over but didn't really want the job. He resigned after a few months and went back to farming. After several months of confusion, Parliament asked Charles I's son – also called Charles – to return to England from abroad to become King. He arrived on 29 May 1660 and immediately insisted that Parliament scrap many of the old Puritan laws. Horse-racing, bear-baiting, theatre visits, football, drinking, Christmas Day and getting your hair cut whenever you wanted were back … and many people in England loved him for it.

Source E ▾ *From a diary by John Evelyn, written in 1658 after the funeral of Oliver Cromwell. Clearly, people didn't take long to start drinking and enjoying themselves again after Cromwell's death!*

> "22 November 1658
>
> It was the joyfullest funeral I ever saw, for there was none that cried but the dogs, which the soldiers hooted away with a barbarous noise, drinking and taking tobacco in the streets as they went."

FACT *Cromwell and the Puritans*

A Civil War had raged in England between the Royalists (led by King Charles I) and Parliament (led by, among others, leading Puritan and MP, Oliver Cromwell) between 1642 and 1648. Parliament won and the King was beheaded. From 1649 onwards, a largely Puritan Parliament ruled England and introduced their laws. Cromwell was a key figure in Parliament and ruled the country himself from 1653 onwards.

WORK

1 What was a Puritan?

2 Copy and complete the table below, listing things that the Puritans banned in the first column and their reasons for banning it in the second.

BANNED BY THE PURITANS	REASONS FOR ITS BAN

3 Look at **Source E**.
   a Why do you think Cromwell's death was being celebrated?
   b What do the actions of some of Cromwell's soldiers tell us about their attitudes to his rule?

4 Read the following statement carefully. 'Governments can create crimes from things that many people consider to be quite acceptable behaviour.'
   a Choose two examples from these four pages that support this view.
   b Choose two modern-day examples that support this statement.

Witch-hunt!

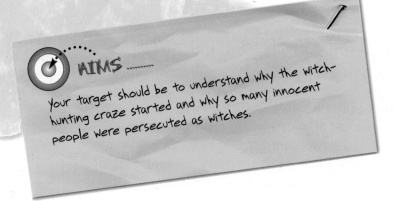

AIMS

Your target should be to understand why the witch-hunting craze started and why so many innocent people were persecuted as witches.

People in Tudor and Stuart England were a very superstitious bunch. The day Queen Elizabeth was crowned, for example, was specially selected only after the stars had been studied for several weeks! Despite the fact that scientists were uncovering more and more about the world, people still didn't understand how animals could suddenly drop down dead or why a field of crops might fail one year. More often than not, when bad things happened in a town or village, it was concluded that a witch was at work. Witches, people thought, were the devil's own helpers, always on the lookout to do evil things and help sinners to find their way to hell!

King James I himself was very interested in witchcraft and even wrote a book, suggesting different ways to catch them. He famously wrote that all witches had strange marks on their bodies where they fed their 'familiars'. A 'familiar' was a small creature – a toad or a cat – that sucked on the witch's blood every night. The 'familiar', James wrote, was really the devil himself in disguise! In fact, all sorts of 'witch-spotting' tips were published – they had no shadow, they talked to themselves, their hair couldn't be cut, they couldn't say the Lord's Prayer without making a mistake and many more.

King James told Parliament to pass strict laws against anybody who was thought to be a witch and, in 1604, witchcraft became a crime punishable by hanging! Over the next one hundred years, thousands of people were accused of witchcraft. Most were poor and, not surprisingly, the majority were old women – after all, they were the most likely to live alone with a pet and have strange marks on their body from a lifetime of hard work!

Source A ▾ *'Swimming' a suspected witch.*

In James I's book, he claimed that a sure-fire way to identify a witch was to 'swim' them. The swimming test, pictured on page 58 in a print from 1612, was a kind of trial. The accused would have their arms tied in front of them and a rope strapped around their waist. They would then be thrown into a pond that would have been 'blessed' by a priest. The test determined that if the accused floated, they must be a witch because the 'pure' water didn't want them. They would be hanged. If they sank, the 'pure' water wanted them so they must be pure themselves and couldn't possibly be a witch – they were declared innocent (but dead!).

The following true story took place at the height of witch fever. It outlines the trial of a 60-year-old widow called *Margaret Harkett* from Stanmore in Middlesex and shows a series of witness statements that led to her execution.

1

Judge: Margaret Harkett of Stanmore, you stand accused of the offence of witchcraft. How do you plead?

Margaret: Not guilty Sir. I'm nothing but a poor, lonely old woman.

2 Witness No.1

Godwin: She called at my farmhouse last year begging for oatmeal. Moments after I refused her, one of my young lambs died. She <u>must</u> have cursed it!

3 Witness No.2

Ball: I know a man who argued with Margaret Harkett, lost his temper and hit her. He went mad soon after. She <u>must</u> have caused this.

4 Witness No.3

Fynde: My husband wouldn't pay her for some shoes she sold him. She just wanted too much for them. Harkett was very angry and muttered something under her breath. A week later, my husband fell out of a tree and died … all because of that witch's curse!

5

Judge: Have you anything to say in your defence Harkett?

Harkett: I'm just a simple old woman wanting a quiet life. There's no proof that I caused all these things to happen — it all sounds like bad luck to me!

6

Judge: I don't agree with you Harkett. It is no coincidence that all these terrible things have happened when people have come into contact with you. I declare you guilty of witchcraft!

7

Margaret Harkett was executed for her 'crimes'. She joined hundreds of others who were killed when 'witch fever' gripped England in the 1600s.

Witch-hunting was at its height in East Anglia during the 14 terrible months between 1645 and 1646. An unsuccessful lawyer named Matthew Hopkins set up his own witch-hunt claiming that he had the devil's own personal list of witches in England. Over two years, hundreds of people were rounded up as a result of his enquiries – and most were old women over the age of 50! He had 68 people put to death in Bury St Edmunds alone and 19 hanged in Chelmsford, Essex, in a single day. In fact, during these years, there were more cases of witchcraft in Essex courts than of any other crime, apart from theft. After Essex, Hopkins set off for Norfolk and Suffolk. The town of Aldeburgh paid him £6 for clearing the town of witches. In King's Lynn, he got £15 and in Stowmarket he received £23. And this was at a time when the average daily wage was two pence!

Source B ▶ *A print from a book of the time featuring Matthew Hopkins. He called himself the 'Witch Finder General' and he is pictured here surrounded by several 'familiars'.*

Source C ▼ *A German painting dated 1555 showing witches burning on a bonfire. The craze for hunting witches never got as bad in England as it did in other countries. Some historians think that around 200 000 people were tortured, burned or hanged for witchcraft in Europe between 1500 and 1750!*

During the seventeenth century, about 2000 people were hanged as witches in England, Wales and Scotland before the 'witch craze' finally began to die down. Witchcraft ceased to be a crime in 1736. England's last victim, Alice Molland, was executed for witchcraft in 1727. Apparently, she had turned her missing daughter into a flying horse!

FACT *Staying dead*

A reminder of the reign of Matthew Hopkins – Witch Finder General – was found in St Osyth County, Essex, in 1921. Two female skeletons were found in a garden, pinned into unmarked graves with large iron staples driven through their bones. This was to make sure that a witch could not return from the grave!

Source D ▾ *Genuine examples of people accused of witchcraft. Each of these people was hanged for their 'crimes'.*

Alice Mulholland: a poor woman who gathered sticks on someone else's land. When told to stop, she threw the sticks down in temper and mumbled something under her breath. Nothing ever grew in that spot again. She was often seen moving her lips in church and could sometimes predict whether it would rain or shine.

Mother Samuel: an old lady who put a spell on two children who were having fits, Samuel claimed they were just naughty boys. The local landowner's wife once tried to cut her hair but Mother Samuel pulled away. The wife began to feel sick.

Thomas Papley: a poor man who owned two vicious cats. He also fed birds. One day, the man's cat frightened a pig. The pig then danced in an odd way and died.

Source E ▾ *This was one of the many ideas for keeping a person safe from a witch's curse. This one was used in Cambridgeshire. Another commonly used idea was to keep a jar full of nail-clippings with a lid on top. Obviously, a witch could be attracted to disgusting things and get trapped in the jar!*

"*Make a black cat spit on sheep's fat,
    then rub the spit inside a horse's hat,
scrape it off within one week,
    then go outside a toad to seek,
and make it sweat into a pot,
    with wooden spoon mix up the lot,
and you will have a healing balm,
    to keep your body free from harm.*"

WISE UP WORD

- magistrate

WORK

1 Look at **Source A**.
   a In your own words, explain how the 'swimming' test was meant to identify a witch.
   b Do you think this was a fair test? Write down the reasons for your answer.

2 Write down five facts about the 'Witch Finder General'.

3 Look at **Source D**.
   a For each of the people in the source, write down the reasons why you think they were accused of being a witch.
   b How would you explain each of the events in the source today?

4 Imagine you are an on-the-spot reporter for a local radio station. You have been asked to cover the trial of Margaret Harkett (page 59) in the 1600s. Write a script for your report, ensuring you include details of her offence, witness statements and the verdict. You may even include your own opinion on matters but remember that you are trying to present this from the point of view of people at the time.

SUMMARY

- Local communities still policed themselves. There was no national police force but, instead, there was a system of local constables, watchmen and the 'hue and cry' to detect and/or stop crime.

- The stocks, pillory and a fines system were still used for minor crimes.

- Punishments were harsh for serious offences and took place in public to frighten others away from committing crimes.

- There were a variety of courts. Royal judges still heard very serious cases but Justices of the Peace (now known as **magistrates** in some areas) were very common, holding 'quarter sessions' four times a year. Church Courts still dealt with churchmen and Manor Courts dealt with local minor crimes, such as drunkenness or selling poor quality goods.

What was the Bloody Code?

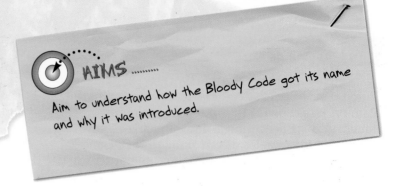

AIMS

Aim to understand how the Bloody Code got its name and why it was introduced.

In 1688, there were 50 crimes punishable by death. By 1765, the number had risen to 160. By the 1800s, they had lost count! There were at least 200 hanging crimes but some experts believe there could have been as many as 350.

These **capital offences** included:

- murder, treason or piracy
- stealing anything worth 25p or more
- cutting down trees in certain areas
- shooting a rabbit
- stealing fish from a river
- forging bank notes
- going around armed in disguise
- stealing anyone who is due to inherit a fortune.

Source A ▼ *An execution at Tyburn by William Hogarth, 1764.*

As a result, hangings were common – and the public really enjoyed them. In London, the executions were carried out at Tyburn (where Marble Arch stands today) and huge crowds gathered to watch as many as five people hanged at a time. So harsh and so frequent were the punishments that the whole legal system became known as the **Bloody Code**. So why had punishment become so 'bloody'?

Reason No 1 *The death penalty was useful*

Lawmakers hoped that tough, public executions for even the most basic of crimes would prevent people from committing them. For centuries, it was widely believed that the best way to stop a crime that was continually committed was to make the punishments harsher and harsher. By killing some of the country's criminals, they were getting rid of them once and for all. Their death prevented them from ever committing crimes again!

Good riddance!

I think I'll replant that tree that I cut down!

Reason No 2 *New crimes were developing*

During the late 1600s and early 1700s, there was a number of 'new' crimes and criminals, which shocked lawmakers into making punishments harsher.

- Vagabonds – unemployment and poverty in the sixteenth century had seen an increase in people wandering around the country looking for work. Some of these men and women turned to crime.

- Highwaymen – slightly better roads and the development of a coaching network meant people travelled around more than ever before. Travellers were easy targets for highwaymen such as Dick Turpin.

Stand and deliver!

I've nothing to deliver, I was going to try to steal from you!

In fact, the first reaction for the lawmakers to any new crime (or a crime they viewed as on the increase) was to make it a capital crime.

Reason No 3 *Many thought crime was on the increase … and were scared!*

It only takes news programmes or newspapers to report several similar crimes over a short period of time to convince the whole country that Britain is riddled with crime! After the invention of printing in the late fifteenth century, a market developed for **broadsheets**, which printed all the ghastly details of violent crimes and painful executions. As a result, many lawmakers genuinely believed that serious crime was on the increase … and responded by introducing more and more capital offences.

Crime is definitely on the increase around here.

Reason No 4 *Lawmakers feared for their property*

The politicians who introduced the laws that made up the Bloody Code were all wealthy landowners or businessmen. Some historians point to the fact that these men used the Bloody Code to protect their own interests. For example, stealing sheep, destroying roads and breaking the tools used to manufacture wool were all punishable by death. It is no coincidence that these crimes are all extremely damaging to a rich landowner who made all his money in the wool trade!

We will protect our country from villains.

Yet this sounds like politicians at the time only cared about themselves. They pointed to the fact that if they protected their businesses with tough punishments, then they protected jobs … and this was beneficial to the whole country.

FACT *Thief taker*

Jonathan Wild was known as the 'thief taker'. People came to him from all over London and paid him to get back their stolen property. His investigations would uncover their goods and he would safely return them to their owners. But Wild had usually organised the robbery in the first place! No wonder he knew how to get the stolen property back! Wild's criminal activities caught up with him eventually. He was trapped by the authorities and convicted of receiving stolen property. He was hanged in 1724.

WORK

1 Write a sentence or two to explain the following phrases: capital offence • Bloody Code

2 Look at **Source A.**
   a What does the source show?
   b Why do you think so many people were attracted to public executions?

3 So why did punishment become so 'bloody' in the eighteenth century? Write a short essay answering this question, emphasising the different reasons why there was a huge increase in capital offences between 1700 and 1850.

WISE UP WORDS

- broadsheet   capital offence   Bloody Code

'Stand and deliver – your money or your life?'

AIMS

- Make sure you know how the Dick Turpin myth differs from the reality.
- Ensure you know at least three factors in both the rise and the fall of the highwayman.

Highwaymen were greatly feared in the late 1600s and early 1700s. **Highway robbery** – using force to steal money or property from travellers on the roads – was not a new crime. However, it was during this period that highwaymen rose to national significance. And one man in particular – Dick Turpin – became so well known that he is now something of a legend.

Image and reality

Today, highwaymen are viewed quite romantically by some as 'gentlemen robbers' – polite, well dressed, charming and clever. They would appear in their masks at the roadside on their beautiful horses and call for the stagecoach driver and his passengers to 'stand [stop] and deliver' any valuables they may have. They rarely used force because most passengers were all too willing to hand over their purses!

The reality of highway robbery was very different. Highwaymen were cruel, violent and greedy, cold-blooded robbers. One highwayman, already wanted for murder, used to cut out the tongues of the people he robbed so they couldn't tell the authorities anything! Travellers sat in fear during long journeys on quiet roads and the government responded to the panic they caused by declaring 'highway robbery' a capital offence.

Source A ▶ *The Dick Turpin story was turned into a series of adventure comics aimed at young children. In this story, Turpin reassures a petrified woman that his partner, Tom King, will look after her while he deals with the other passengers. Over the years, Turpin's story has inspired romantic novels, plays, films, a TV series and even pop songs (ask your teacher about Adam Ant!).*

ONE PENNY.

DICK TURPIN

Nº 14

YOUR MONEY OR YOUR LIFE!

"Fear not, young lady," said Dick Turpin, "no harm shall come to you. I have a villain to deal with, but he shall have fair play. I pray you walk a short distance with my friend, Tom King." Half drawing his sword, Sir Grayson staggered back against the carriage.

So who was Dick Turpin?

Dick Turpin lived between 1705 and 1739. A hundred years after his death, a poem about him glamorised his crimes and included a story about him riding his horse, Black Bess, all the way from London to York in record time to provide himself with an **alibi** for a crime he had committed. A few years later, the poem was turned into a musical … and then a series of cheap comics – the Dick Turpin legend was born! Turpin was also known for other things:

- he was said to be very handsome and incredibly brave;
- he robbed only the richest people's stagecoaches and was always very polite … especially to the young ladies!

But the real Dick Turpin was a stark contrast to his image. He worked as a butcher before joining a gang of robbers to make more money. As well as stealing cattle, they broke into houses, tortured the occupants and stole all their cash. Turpin turned to highway robbery after most of his 'crew' were arrested. He joined with Tom King and spent two years terrorising travellers in Essex.

In 1739, he was arrested for horse stealing but the authorities didn't know who he was. From jail he wrote to his brother but his old teacher recognised his handwriting and informed local magistrates. He was hanged in York in May 1739, aged 34.

Source B ▼ *From J B Le Blanc's* Letters on the English and French Nations, *1737.*

> "Your friend, Mr Colling, was surprised last year near Cambridge by the famous Turpin. The highwayman, having repeated in chain the command to stand, fired at him. Although the shot missed him, Mr Colling decided to obey. Turpin took his money, his watch and his snuff box, leaving him only two shillings to continue his journey."

WISE UP WORDS

- alibi   highway robbery

Source C ▼ *From* The Newgate Calendar, *a newspaper, 1737.*

> "A reward of £100 had been offered for Turpin's capture. Thomas Morris, a keeper in Epping Forest, accompanied by a pedlar [a salesman], set off to catch him. Turpin saw them approaching and noticed that Morris was carrying a gun and thought he was a poacher. Turpin said he'd 'find no rabbits in this part of the forest'. 'No' said Morris, 'but I've found a Turpin'. Raising his gun, he told Turpin to surrender. Turpin spoke to him in a friendly way and gradually retreated, till, having seized his own gun, he shot Morris dead. The pedlar ran off quickly."

WORK

1 Write a sentence or two to explain the following words or phrases: highway robbery • stand and deliver

2 a Who was Dick Turpin?

  b In what way does the legend of Dick Turpin differ from the reality?

3 Below is a list of factors that either:

  i) explain the development of highway robbery in the 1700s; or

  ii) explain its decline.

  a Sort the ten factors into two lists. The first list should explain the developments and the second should explain the decline of highway robbers.

  b For each factor, explain how it either allows highway robbery to develop or contributes to its downfall.

- Guns became easier and cheaper to get.
- There was no police force to track down highway robbers.
- Road patrols were set up around major cities.
- Horses became cheaper to buy.
- High rewards were offered for the capture of highwaymen.
- People used banks more and didn't carry as much cash around with them.
- Coaching became big business with lots of coaches travelling around the country every day.
- There was lots of open land around towns in which highwaymen could operate.
- Taverns that were used by highwaymen were closed down.
- There was less open land around towns as it was used to build on.

'Brandy for the Parson, 'baccy for the Clerk'

AIMS ....

Try to remember reasons why people smuggled goods into Britain and why the smuggling trade declined in the late 1700s.

Before you start this double page, write down or discuss what the word 'smuggling' means. What words or phrases spring to mind when the word 'smuggling' is mentioned or what examples of 'smuggling' can you note down?

Smuggling is a crime entirely invented by politicians and governments. During the seventeenth and eighteenth centuries, the British government collected huge sums of money in the form of **import duties** – taxes paid on goods like tea, cloth, wine and tobacco brought in by ships from overseas.

These taxes – as much as 30% – made the items very expensive, so smuggling them in and avoiding paying the tax became big business. A smuggled bottle of brandy from France was much cheaper to buy (and therefore easier to sell) than a bottle on which duty had been paid!

Who smuggled?

Smugglers operated all along Britain's coast but were most common on the south coast, just a night's sail from France. Thousands of people were involved. According to court records in 1748, of the 103 people officially wanted for smuggling, over 70% of them were farm workers – they could make nearly ten times as much in one night from smuggling than they could working for a week in the fields!

Source A ▾ *Part of A Smuggler's Song by Rudyard Kipling. The warning in the poem for anyone to 'watch the wall' and avoid looking at the smugglers was probably sound advice. Large smuggling gangs were formed all over the south coast – and they weren't afraid to use violence to avoid capture and keep their identities a secret.*

> "Five and twenty ponies
> Trotting through the dark –
> Brandy for the Parson.
> 'Baccy for the Clerk;
> Laces for a lady, letters for a spy,
> And watch the wall, my darling, while
> the Gentlemen go by!"

Source B ▾ *Smugglers land their cargo.*

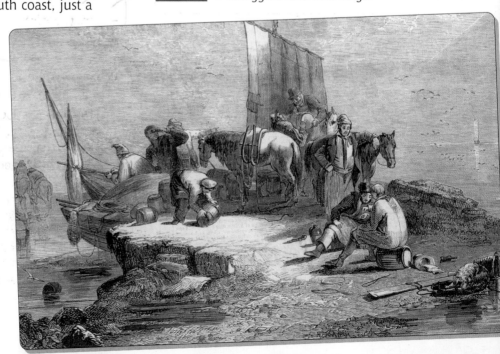

Why smuggle?

Smuggling was a good way to make money for the smugglers … and their customers were always ready to buy cheaper goods than they could find at their local market. Many ordinary people became involved in smuggling – they left barn doors open or cellars unlocked and didn't ask too many questions about the goods kept in there. Many tradesmen too – tobacco sellers, wine merchants, cloth salesmen – took advantage of the cheaper 'smuggled in' goods to sell in their shops. In short, many ordinary citizens just didn't regard smuggling as a crime. They saw smuggling as 'victimless' because they felt the only people to suffer were the government who made less money in taxes!

FACT *'Slippery Sam'*

One of Britain's most famous smugglers was Samuel Jackson AKA 'Slippery Sam'. He received and distributed contraband all along the south coast and had a warren of tunnels underneath a house he bought near Canterbury that enabled him to come and go as he pleased. He earned his nickname when he covered himself in grease and slipped through the iron bars of Maidstone Jail after he was arrested one night. At the age of 30, after shooting and killing a tax officer, Sam was caught and hanged in 1760. His body was displayed until it rotted as a warning to others!

FACT *Poaching*

Poaching means stealing wild creatures, live birds or fish from those who own the land or water in which they live. There were tough punishments for poachers in the 1700s, such as the 1723 Black Act that said anyone caught hunting with a 'blackened face' could be executed. Possessing dogs or poaching equipment could mean a year in prison too. Many hated the poaching laws. Who owns wild creatures anyway? It meant that farmers couldn't kill rabbits that ate their corn or hungry farm workers couldn't catch a fish to feed their families. But not all poachers were poaching to eat – some made lots of money selling their 'catch' at the local market – so should we feel sorry for poachers at all?

Smuggling and the Bloody Code

As you might expect, the crime of smuggling was punishable by death under the Bloody Code. But the threat of death if caught clearly didn't stop the smugglers. In fact, one official report recorded that three million pounds of tea was smuggled into Britain each year, *three times* as much as was legally imported!

In the 1780s, Prime Minister William Pitt lowered the taxes on imported foods. As a result, smuggling became less profitable. Taxes were lowered further in the nineteenth century and the level of smuggling seen one hundred years before finally came to an end.

Source C ▾ *Adapted from a letter by the Duke of Richmond, written in 1749.*

> "The common people of this country do not regard smuggling as a crime. So what can the government do to punish the guilty? Accessories [those who assist in smuggling or let it go on without stopping it] should be punished as well as the smugglers for you know very well that the feeling in the country is that a man may stand by and see crimes committed and even assist in them and be unpunished if he doesn't commit the crime with his own hands!"

WISE UP WORD

- import duties

WORK

It is 1750 and the government is worried about the growth of smuggling. They have asked you to write a secret report. Ensure you answer the following key questions in your report:

- Which goods are smuggled?
- How much is smuggled?
- Who is involved in the smuggling 'trade'?
- Why do people become smugglers?
- How well organised are the smugglers?
- And, in your opinion, what is the best way to prevent the continued growth of the smuggling trade?

Case study: Transportation

AIMS ....

After studying these four pages, make sure you are clear about:

• why transportation was used as a punishment;
• the impact of transportation on the criminal and the receiving countries;
• why transportation ended as a punishment in 1868.

In May 1787, 11 ships left Portsmouth, heading for the 'new' British colony of Australia. There were 1020 people in total. 736 of them were convicted criminals sentenced to spend seven years, fourteen years or life in this hot, baron wilderness known by many as 'the place beyond the seas'. This punishment was known as **transportation** and over 160 000 people were sent to Australia as a punishment between 1787 and 1868.

So why did the British government introduce transportation to Australia? Who was transported? What happened when prisoners got there? And was transportation a successful form of punishment … or not?

That first voyage took over eight months and fifty people died on the way. The oldest convict was an 82-year-old woman called Dorothy Handland. She survived the trip but hanged herself from a tree when she saw the conditions in which she was expected to live. John Hudson had stolen some clothes and a gun and became the youngest to be transported. He was nine years old. Soon the convicts began to build their settlement. Each person was assigned a master who used the convict to carry out whatever work they wanted for the remainder of their sentence. Good, hard-working convicts earned themselves an early release whilst bad behaviour ended in a flogging. Over the next 20 years, the British courts sent over 20 000 convicts to join them.

Source A ▶ *A copy of a warning sign on an old bridge, Sturminster, Dorset.*

So why was transportation to Australia introduced?

• Transportation itself had been used as a punishment since the early 1700s. Convicts often found themselves sent to America, Bermuda or Gibraltar. When America won its independence, it obviously refused to accept any more British criminals. Another colony was desperately needed and Australia seemed to fit the bill; it had been mapped and claimed as a British territory in 1770.

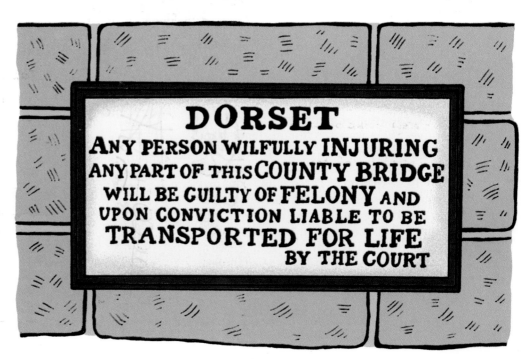

DORSET
ANY PERSON WILFULLY INJURING ANY PART OF THIS COUNTY BRIDGE WILL BE GUILTY OF FELONY AND UPON CONVICTION LIABLE TO BE TRANSPORTED FOR LIFE BY THE COURT

- Transportation was seen as a useful alternative to hanging. In the early 1800s, there were over 200 crimes that could be punished by a death sentence. Yet many judges were not happy about hanging people for minor crimes. They were far happier 'transporting' a person instead. It was seen as a 'middle punishment' between the harsh reality of hanging and the milder sanction of public whipping or a fine.

- Transportation was used often because it reduced crime by completely removing the criminals who were committing it. It was hoped that if the convict came back, they would have learned useful skills when they were forced to work in order to survive.

- Government officials hoped too, that by filling one of their colonies with thousands of tough Brits, it would stop other countries – like France – from trying to 'muscle in' and take control of Australia and her resources.

Source B ▾ *A selection of convict records from Nottingham Borough Courthouse, 1822–1852.*

- **JAMES CLAY** – 16 JANUARY 1822 – TRANSPORTED FOR SEVEN YEARS FOR STEALING MATHEMATICS EQUIPMENT.
- **ROBERT DEPLIDGE** – 15 JANUARY 1829 – TRANSPORTED FOR SEVEN YEARS FOR STEALING TWO PIGS.
- **MEGAN LEACH** – 29 JUNE 1831 – TRANSPORTED FOR 14 YEARS FOR STEALING THREE DUCKS.
- **THOMAS ALLSOPP** – 10 APRIL 1833 – TRANSPORTED FOR SEVEN YEARS FOR STEALING ONE PAIR OF SHOES.
- **JAMES MORRIS** – 25 JUNE 1840 – TRANSPORTED FOR LIFE FOR STEALING VARIOUS GOODS FROM THOMAS DAWSON.
- **JOSEPH ASHWORTH** – 6 APRIL 1841 – TRANSPORTED FOR SEVEN YEARS FOR STEALING FOUR PENNIES FROM JEMIMA TAYLOR.
- **MATTHEW CUFF** – 31 DECEMBER 1846 – TRANSPORTED FOR SEVEN YEARS FOR STEALING A DONKEY.
- **THOMAS ATKINSON** – 1 JULY 1852 – TRANSPORTED FOR SEVEN YEARS FOR BREAKING AND ENTERING INTO THE SHOP OF HIS MASTER AND STEALING 108 HATS, 6 UMBRELLAS AND 60 HANDKERCHIEFS.

Source C ▾ *A typical convict.*

Age
- Average age of convict - 27

Sex
- About 15% of convicts were women

Food
- Breakfast - porridge
- Lunch - bread, pound of salted meat
- Dinner - bread, cup of tea

Crimes
- 80% of transported convicts were thieves; most had been convicted several times
- About 5% had been transported for violent crimes

Nationality
- 70% English and welsh
- 25% Irish
- 5% Scottish

Where
- Majority had been brought up in a town or city

Source D ▾ *Prisoners awaiting transportation to Australia at Chatham Docks, 1828. Note the **hulks** – disused warships – that were used to transport the men and women. Conditions on these rotting vessels were often terrible, with death rates as high as one in three on some voyages.*

Source F ▾ *A chart demonstrating the growth and eventual decline of transportation.*

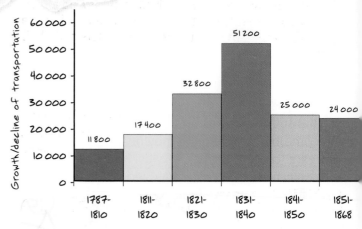

Source G ▾ *Convicts in Tasmania, an island near to Australia. Here they are undergoing a sentence of 'hard labour'. They are made to carry 50 kilos (as heavy as 50 bags of sugar) for up to 30 miles.*

Source E ▾ *From Peter Moss' History Alive 3.*

"For lesser offences – say, killing a rabbit or taking turnips from a farmer's field – the prisoner could be transported for 5, 7 or 14 years. This meant a dreadful voyage in a prison ship to the new colony of Australia, or later Bermuda or Gibraltar, where the convict became a slave. He worked as an unpaid servant to one of the settlers or else as a labourer in a chain gang making roads and buildings for the government. Many ex-convicts managed to return to England illegally, but if they were caught, they were liable to be executed."

FACT *Wipe out!*

The first convicts arrived in Tasmania in 1802. Over 20 000 native Tasmanians lived there already. Just 75 years later, the last native Tasmanian died – a whole nation wiped out by British rulers and their brutal convicts.

Source H ▾ *A Certificate of Freedom issued to Francis Mill in Sydney, Australia, 1838. If convicts behaved themselves, their sentence could be reduced or ended by one of these certificates or **tickets of leave**.*

The majority of convicts decided to stay in Australia at the end of their sentences, realising that they could probably make a better life there rather than returning to Britain. Prisoners who had served their sentences and stayed found that wages were higher in Australia than they were 'back home'. By the mid-1800s, transportation was even seen as more of an opportunity than a punishment by many people in Britain. When gold was discovered in 1851, thousands of people in Britain actually began paying to travel on the ships bound for Australia in order to seek their fortune. Soon, Australians began objecting to their country being used as a dumping ground for Britain's criminals. Transportation ended in 1868.

WORK

1 Why was transportation introduced? Explain at least three reasons in detail.

2 Make your own copy of **Source C**, remembering to include all the labels. Give your diagram the title 'So who was transported to Australia?'

3 What sort of life awaited a transported convict upon arrival overseas?

4 What was a ticket of leave?

5 Why was transportation eventually ended?

SUMMARY

• There was no police force, and local communities and towns were expected to police themselves. The 'hue and cry' system was still used and constables patrolled the streets. Thief takers made their living from tracking down criminals and collecting rewards.

• Hundreds of crimes carried the death penalty. This was known as the 'Bloody Code'. However, far fewer people were hanged than should have been. Juries often took pity on young children and said that they were not guilty rather than have them killed!

• There was a variety of courts – royal judges heard serious cases whilst magistrates (formerly known as Justices of the Peace) held trials four times a year (known as quarter sessions). Church Courts still dealt with churchmen and Manor Courts were still helped by local lords and dealt with minor crimes.

Have you been learning?

TASK 1: ANAGRAMS

In the word box below, you will find:

- Tudor tramps
- beggar talk
- home of torture
- confession by a stretch
- banned in 1652
- strict Protestants
- Matthew Hopkins
- tough legal system
- famous highwayman
- sent abroad
- brought in from abroad
- tried to investigate crimes, gather information and hold trials.

All the answers are given below, but the words and letters have been mixed up. Can you unravel them?

> tpasnrtonartio • kidc pruint
> • gmnugsgil
> • ydrstu grsaegb • itanncg
> • ihcwt dfrnei earnlge
> • wrote fo nnoold • siarthcsm
> • cark • iutrpnsa
> • eucisjt fo het aeepc
> • ldyobo ecdo

TASK 2: TORTURE IN THE TOWER

1581.—Cuthbert Simpson on the Rack. (Being a portion of the Cut representing his sufferings Fox's 'Acts and Monuments.'

a Describe, in as much detail as you can, what is going on in this picture.
b What other forms of torture were used at this time? You should be able to list two or three examples.
c Why were people tortured like this?
d Why do you think we don't torture suspected criminals like this today?

TASK 3: NAUGHTY GEORGE

Look at this 'wanted' poster for George Pearse, then answer the questions that follow. Note that the letter 's' looked a lot like the letter 'f'.

Source A

11ᵗʰ MAY, 1761.

Broke out of his Majesty's Goal,

At *Wilton*, near *Taunton*, in the County of *Somerfet* ; in the Night, between the *Nineteenth* and *Twentieth* Days of *April* laft, with two other Prifoners fince Re-taken,

GEORGE PEARSE;

Committed for Returning from Tranfportation before the Time limited.

THE faid GEORGE PEARSE is about fixty Years Old, and five Feet five Inches High ; has a large Face ; a flat Mouth, which, when he Speaks, is drawn rather to one fide of his Face. He has loft all his fore Teeth, and ftammers in his Speech ; leans very forward in Walking ; his Legs bending outwards ; has Black Hair, which hangs loofe about his Ears : Speaks Lifping, and had on (when he went away) an old Blue Coat, Leather Breeches, and White Stockings.———He pretends to be a Farrier, and to underftand and Cure Diforders in *Bullocks* and *Sheep* ; and generally carries with him fome Papers, fhowing what Cures he pretends to have Wrought on Cattle.

HE was born at *Withypoole*, in the County aforefaid.

Whoever Re-takes and Secures the faid GEORGE PEARSE, (fo as he may be brought back again to the faid Goal) fhall receive *Three Guineas* Reward, with all Reafonable Expences, of GEORGE STRONG, Keeper of the faid Goal ; and all Magiftrates and Peace-Officers, are earneftly defired to Search for the faid Delinquent, in their feveral Precincts.

NORTON, near TAUNTON : Printed by J. PILE.

---

1 **a** From which prison had George escaped?
 b When did he escape?
 c How many prisoners escaped with him?
 d Have they caught the other prisoners yet?
 e Why had George been put in prison in the first place?
 f How much is the reward for George's capture in modern currency (1 guinea = £1.05)?

2 **a** According to the poster, what might George's occupation be?
 b The poster was issued three weeks after George's escape. Why do you think the authorities delayed the poster?
 c How does this 'wanted' poster differ from a modern one?

TASK 4: SUMMARY

Draw a table like the one below and use your knowledge of crime and punishment in Medieval England and Tudor and Stuart England to complete it.

	MEDIEVAL ENGLAND	TUDOR AND STUART ENGLAND	IN YOUR OPINION, DID THINGS CHANGE OR STAY THE SAME?
LAWS			
POLICING			
TRIALS			
PUNISHMENTS			

TASK 5: QUESTION TIME

Look at these genuine GCSE questions carefully. Why not try to complete them as a revision exercise? In brackets after each question, you will find the pages of this book where there is information that might refresh your memory.

- Briefly explain the main features of the eighteenth-century Bloody Code. (pages 62–71)

- Was smuggling an easy, or a difficult, crime for the authorities to deal with? Explain your answer. (pages 66–67)

How did life change during the Industrial Revolution?

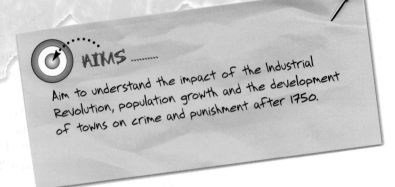

⊙ AIMS ....

Aim to understand the impact of the Industrial Revolution, population growth and the development of towns on crime and punishment after 1750.

The greatest ever change to life in Britain occurred during the period 1750–1900. It was known as the Industrial Revolution. The changes affected all parts of British society and altered the way people lived their lives. They affected crime and punishment too!

Towns

About seven million people lived in Britain in 1750. Most lived and worked in villages or small towns. There were few big cities. By 1900, the population had grown to nearly 40 million. The majority now lived in crowded towns and cities full of disease and poor-quality housing.

Source A ⚊ *Slums showing back-to-back housing. In 1850, the writer Charles Reade described Sheffield as 'perhaps the most hideous town in creation ... sparkling streams entered the town ... but soon got filthy, full of rubbish, clogged with dirt and bubbling with rotten, foul-smelling gases.'*

Source B ⚊ *From a modern historian.*

"The terrible poverty and the conditions in the slums caused crime and violence. There were parts of most cities where strangers would not dare to go out, especially after dark. Robbery and murder were committed even in the 'better' streets. The old village-type of policing was not adequate for towns."

Source C ⚊ *Inside a factory in the nineteenth century.*

Work

In 1750, about 80% of people worked in the countryside, mainly on farms. By 1900, about 80% worked in factories in towns and cities.

Source D ▾ *This quote is based on the words of John Stone of Leicester who was defending an accusation of stealing a watch in 1822. Stone and his father used to work in a small workshop next to their home in a village near Leicestershire. The factories in the city now made the cloth much cheaper (and quicker) and put his family out of work.*

"I am a poor weaver in distress. I was travelling into Leicestershire, having been to London to offer myself as a soldier but I wasn't tall enough. My parents are poor, my father out of work. I have eight brothers and sisters."

Politics and protest

In 1750, only 5% of the male population could vote … and no women. Demands for change were made at a large meeting. At one political 'rally' in Manchester in 1819, government troops killed 11 people. Many other riots and protests occurred over such things as food prices, toll road charges and the introduction of new machines that replaced ordinary labourers. By 1900, many changes had taken place and nearly all men were able to vote. However, women still couldn't vote and some started their own violent protest movement soon after.

Source E ▾ *A modern historian describes a link between changing work practices, as a result of the Industrial Revolution, and crime. From* In Search of History, 1714–1900.

"In the Midlands, there was a big cottage industry in knitting. In 1800, a hand knitter could earn up to £1.35 a week. But factory owners were installing new machines that could make wider cloth. This was then cut up to make stockings … the cottage workers just could not compete; wages fell sharply, while food costs were rising. So the cottage workers fought back. In 1811, organised gangs set about smashing new machines. In one year alone, they destroyed about 1000 of them."

New ideas

In the years after 1700, more and more philosophers and thinkers began to view the human race differently. Some thought that with better education, living and working conditions, human beings could behave far more responsibly. Some went so far as saying that the purpose of punishment should be to change the criminal for the better rather than to humiliate them. These new ideas would soon have an impact on crime and punishment.

Source F ▾ *A modern historian discusses the purpose of punishment.*

"In the nineteenth century, the main purpose of punishment was to reform the criminal, rather than to warn others away from crime. Punishments took place in private, not public. The aim was to change the prisoner rather than just getting rid of them."

Source G ▾ *From Peter Moss' History Alive 1789–1914.*

"Fortunately, a few clear-sighted men saw that savage punishment was not the answer to crime. They realised it was much better to catch more criminals and give them light sentences than to let 99 out of every 100 escape and to punish the hundredth by execution. Some men and women realised that terrible conditions in prisons, far from reforming the convicts, only made them worse than ever."

WORK

1 What do you understand by the term Industrial Revolution? Write out your own definition.

2 Look at **Sources A** and **B**. How might poverty be linked to an increase in crime?

3 Look at **Sources D** and **E**. How might changes in work be linked with crime?

4 Look at **Sources F** and **G**. According to these sources, how did some people begin to change their views on crime and punishment during the nineteenth century?

The petition of James Hillier, 1821

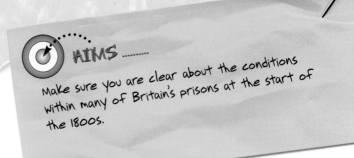

AIMS ....

Make sure you are clear about the conditions within many of Britain's prisons at the start of the 1800s.

Not all convicted criminals were hanged or transported overseas. During the late 1700s and 1800s, thousands of convicted men, woman and children were sent to one of Britain's fast-growing prisons where conditions were extremely harsh. One prisoner, a 25-year-old man named James Hillier, was so upset by his treatment in prison that he wrote to Parliament begging them to change the way prisons were run. So what did his letter say? What had driven him to write? And how bad, exactly, were Britain's prisons at the start of the 1800s?

Source A ▼ Letter from James Hillier to the House of Commons.

"I am in jail at Ilchester, under a sentence of 18 months, for stealing in a shop in Bristol. In February, another prisoner and I were playing at hustle-cap [a gambling game] for a few pennies and we squabbled about it. Another prisoner, called Penny, reported me to the Governor [the jail manager] for playing hustle-cap and I was placed in heavy double irons, twice doubled, so that I couldn't move my legs more than nine inches apart; handcuffs were then placed upon me and my hands and feet were chained together. I was literally chained down. I was then dragged away and thrown into a cold, damp, dark dungeon where I remained until the next day. Then I was dragged in front of a visiting magistrate and another gentleman who laughed at me, then led back to the cell again where I remained for nine days and nights. I couldn't put my hands to my mouth, stand upright or lie straight unless it was when the chain was taken off. This was done for one hour every day to allow me to eat bread and answer the calls of nature. For the remaining 23 hours a day, I remained in distress and pain for nine days and nights. My arms swelled up with the pressure of handcuffs so much that they were buried in my flesh. When the guard came to take them off, he had to use lots of force to get them out of my flesh and he laughed at my sufferings.

I therefore pray that the Honourable House takes my sufferings into consideration and, if you don't give me any relief for my sufferings, at least take measure to protect us from such cruel and inhumane treatment in the future.

X" [The mark of James Hillier. He couldn't write so he got someone to do it for him and he put a cross as a mark for his name.]

In Britain's prisons, convicts of all ages were packed into filthy cells without enough water, food, toilets or light. The men who looked after them – the jailers – didn't earn a wage so made their money by hiring beds and blankets to the prisoners and selling them food, beer, tobacco and extra clothing. If prisoners didn't have any money, they relied on local charities that gave them the odd dirty blanket and a pennyworth of bread a day.

Wealthy prisoners could live in luxury – fancy beds, expensive clothing, fine wines and tasty food items could be purchased from the jailer. And no one could leave prison, even if found innocent, until they'd paid a 'jailer's fee'. Innocent people then were kept in prison for years because they couldn't afford the fee to be let out. Those people who owed money – debtors – were often joined by their families until they paid what they owed. Some stayed inside for the rest of their lives!

Source B ▶ *Statistics on those people held in jail in 1776. From a survey by John Howard.*

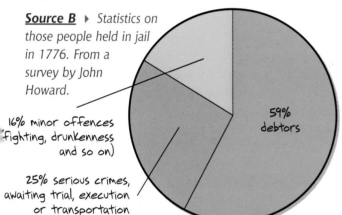

16% minor offences (fighting, drunkenness and so on)

25% serious crimes, awaiting trial, execution or transportation

59% debtors

Source C ▾ *From a report on Newgate Prison, 1814. Remember debtors had committed no other crime, except being unable to pay their debts.*

"No bedding is provided: the poorer description of prisoners sleep on the boards between two rugs given by the city. Those who can afford it hire beds at sixpence a night. The allowance of food for debtors is 14 ounces of bread a day and eight stone of meat divided among all [this amounted to about two ounces a day per person – just a bit heavier than a pen, pencil and ruler]: there are no candles or coals, no maps or buckets…"

Source D ▾ *A report from an area of a prison where most prisoners were women.*

"The women's yards … with cells are calculated for seventy people. In January last, 130 were, at one time, crowded together of all ages, all descriptions, tried and untried; and even those under sentence of death not removed … amongst these now are two girls of thirteen, one of twelve and one of ten years old."

Source E ▾ *The breakdown of guilty sentences in Britain in 1830.*

In 1830, of every eight prisoners found guilty:

one was sentenced to death

two were transported

five were sent to prison

Source F ▾ *An artist's impression of life in prison for James Hillier.*

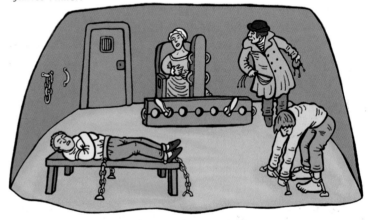

WORK

1 Look at **Source A**.
  a To whom did James Hillier send his petition?
  b Why had he been sent to prison in the first place?
  c Why had Hillier been placed in double irons?
  d How long was he kept in double irons?
  e What action did Hillier want Parliament to take?

2 a Prepare a fact file entitled 'The state of prisons, 1800', containing information about staffing, prisoners and accommodation. Your fact file should contain at least ten facts about the problems of the prisons.
  b For each of the problems you have highlighted in your fact file, suggest a solution.

Why did prisons change?

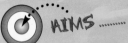

AIMS

Aim to understand:
- the impact of reformers like Elizabeth Fry and John Howard;
- how prisons changed during the 1800s;
- the difference between the silent and separate systems ... and the reasons for their use.

In the early 1800s, a visit to a prison would have been a very harrowing (and smelly) experience. Due to the lack of proper water supply or sewage systems, visitors used handkerchiefs soaked in vinegar so they couldn't smell the prisoners. About a quarter of prisoners died each year from disease and typhus (a virus spread by mites, lice and fleas) was so common it was nicknamed 'jail fever'. A survey showed that of the 4000 people in prison in the whole country, over 60% were there because they owed money ... and because they couldn't get out until they'd paid their debts, many stayed there until they died! Like debtors, many in the prisons were not there as a punishment. Instead, they were kept there until their punishment (hanging, whipping, stocks and so on) was carried out. There were different sorts of jail too – towns and counties ran some, while private individuals managed others, sometimes with no rules!

By the 1870s, things had changed massively. Imprisonment had become the normal method of punishing criminals whilst turning the prisoners themselves into reformed characters had become an accepted aim of prison life. Government inspectors even checked prisoners' diets, health and living conditions. So why did prisons change?

During the eighteenth century, most people accepted that prisons were awful places. They believed that a person in prison was most likely a bad person, so why should they be treated well? But some people disagreed!

One of them was John Howard, a sheriff from Bedfordshire who was responsible for all the prisons in his county. He made tours of prisons across Britain and abroad and was so shocked by what he saw that he published his findings in a book called *The State of Prisons in England and Wales* in 1777. He also gave evidence to Parliament.

Source A ▾ *A summary of John Howard's book. Eventually, all his proposals were introduced.*

The State of Prisons in England and Wales, 1777

FINDINGS

- Disease is common.
- There aren't enough people employed to look after the prisoners.
- The jailers earn no wage so make their money by charging the prisoners for food and bedding.
- Many prisoners learn more about crime from other prisoners.
- Many prisoners found innocent cannot afford the jailers' fees to be let out ... so stay inside!

RECOMMENDATIONS

- Clean running water.
- Prison doctors appointed.
- Food for all prisoners.
- The end of fees paid to jailers.
- Regular visits by churchmen.
- Prisoners to work hard and spend lots of time in silence so they can change their attitudes to crime.

John Howard was not alone in visiting the country's prisons. Some people actually went in to help. One was a woman named Elizabeth Fry who first visited London's Newgate Prison in 1813. She was so shocked by the filthy conditions that she spent the rest of her life trying to improve things for prisoners. She encouraged them to clean up their cells and found them work knitting socks. She is probably most famous for helping women prisoners to read and write. She began a school for prisoners' children and held Bible readings.

Source B ▼ *Fry's work was so well-respected that, in 2002, she was chosen by the Bank of England to go on their new £5 note.*

Some laughed at Fry's efforts but she did influence people's views on prison life. By the 1820s and 1830s, reformers in Parliament too had realised that the terrible conditions in prisons, far from reforming the convicts, only made them worse than ever. A Jail Act of 1823, proposed by the Home Secretary, Robert Peel, began a long series of reforms that laid the foundations of our modern prison service.

FACT *Prison names*

Criminals have invented many nicknames for prison over the years. They include: the can, chokey, clanger, clink, cooler, coup, inside, nick, pen, pokey, slammer and tronk.

Source C ▼ *The 1823 Jail Act. To the amazement of many who believed that the harsher the punishment, the better it would be, this milder treatment led to fewer men returning to prison.*

THE JAIL ACT, 1823

- PRISONS MUST BE SECURE AND HEALTHY.
- JAILERS ARE TO BE PAID BY THE GOVERNMENT.
- MAGISTRATES ARE TO VISIT PRISONS.
- FEMALE PRISONERS ARE TO BE KEPT SEPARATE FROM MEN AND HAVE FEMALE WARDENS.
- DOCTORS AND CHURCHMEN ARE TO VISIT PRISONS REGULARLY.
- TEACHERS ARE TO BE EMPLOYED.
- ATTEMPTS MUST BE MADE TO REFORM PRISONERS.

'Silent versus separate'

One of the biggest debates in the 1800s involved how to treat prisoners once in jail. Two ideas were tried: the **silent system** and the **separate system**.

Silent: involved a prisoner doing a boring task in complete silence. They were forced to walk around 'treadmills' like hamsters in a cage, unravel old rope or turn handles that scooped up and emptied cups of sand. The idea was to allow a prisoner time to reflect on their crime … and not allow them any chance to corrupt each other.

I feel more like a hamster every day!

Separate: this was solitary confinement in the prisoner's own cell. After weeks of non-contact, the prison chaplain would persuade the prisoner to lead a better, godlier life. Pentonville Prison opened in 1842 as a model 'separate prison' and by 1850, there were 50 others using the system. But some critics said that 'separate' was too tough. Suicide rates were high because prisoners were driven mad by loneliness. And there was no evidence that it reformed prisoners either. The separate system was very expensive (new prisons had to be built!) and over time, solitary confinement became an extra punishment rather than the normal way of prison life.

FACT *Tough love!*

Prisons were finally brought under direct government control in 1878. During that year, the man in charge of all prisons was quoted as saying 'a prisoner's life should consist of hard labour, hard beds and hard food.'

WISE UP WORDS

- separate system   silent system

Source D ▾ *From an 1861 book describing the silent and separate systems.*

"The silent system is applied to a number of prisoners, varying from 40 to 80. They are seated upon benches, about three metres apart, all facing in the direction of the officer's desk. All pick cotton, except a few who are undergoing the punishment of compulsory idleness. At meals, the same order is observed.

The discipline is not merely that the silence of the tongue is observed. No sign, no look is permitted, nor is it often attempted. A prisoner, recently committed and not quite sober, once started up with 'Britons never should be slaves'. A quiet smile on the face of some of the old jail-birds was the only result: not a single head was turned while he was removed from the room.

As a general rule, a few months in the separate cell makes the prisoner easily persuaded. The chaplain can then make the brawny prisoner cry like a child; he can work on his feelings in almost any way he pleases. He can, so to speak, photograph his own thoughts, wishes and opinions on his patient's mind and fill his mouth with his own phrases and language."

Source E ▾ *Coldbath Fields was known as a tough prison. It was rebuilt in 1794 and then extended again and again. The grey shading shows old building; the pink shows building that was new when this plan was made in 1884.*

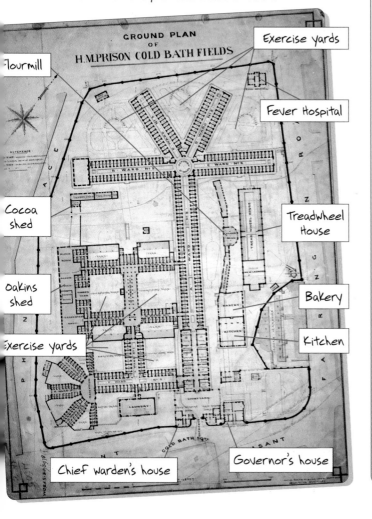

Source F ▾ *Some key dates in prison reform.*

1820 – Flogging of women ended.

1835 – Prison inspectors appointed.

1839 – General rules for all prisons provided by the government.

1842 – Pentonville Prison built, a model prison for others to copy. It kept the prisoners in permanent isolation from each other.

1852 – Transportation of women ended.

1857 – Government ends using hulks (old boats) as prisons.

1864 – Penal Servitude Act introduced. Conditions got tougher and whippings and electric shocks were introduced for prisoners not working hard enough. This was the response to the outcry (largely started by newspapers) over a wave of robberies in the early 1860s. An MP was strangled and robbed in 1862 and the press blamed prisoners who had won early release for good behaviour!

1878 – Government took control of all prisoners.

WORK

1 **a** Why did visitors to prisons use handkerchiefs soaked in vinegar?

   b What is a debtor?

   c Why were prisons so unhealthy?

2 Write a paragraph explaining how John Howard and Elizabeth Fry contributed to the improvement of prison life.

3 **a** In your own words, explain: i) the silent system; ii) the separate system.

   b Which, if either, of the two systems do you think was best for: i) the prisoners; ii) the people who ran the prisons?

4 Look at **Source E**.

   a Find: the old prison, the new prison, the Treadwheel House, the flourmill, the bakery, the kitchen, the oakins shed, the governor's house, the Fever Hospital, the exercise yards, the cocoa shed and the chief warden's house.

   b The prison was designed logically. Explain the placing of: the Fever Hospital, the new prison, the Treadwheel House, the flourmill and the governor's house.

George and Elizabeth

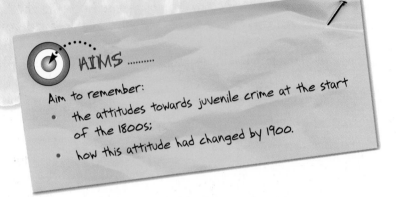

AIMS ....

Aim to remember:
- the attitudes towards juvenile crime at the start of the 1800s;
- how this attitude had changed by 1900.

Child crime has always been a great issue in Britain. Today, you will always hear newspaper and television stories about 'youth crime' or 'yob culture'. Child crime was one of the big concerns in Victorian society too. Over the next two pages, you will be introduced to two young criminals – George and Elizabeth – and encouraged to look at how Victorian society punished their crimes. For centuries, young offenders had been treated in exactly the same ways as older criminals. They received the same punishments and found themselves in the same prisons. In 1830, a boy of nine was hanged for setting fire to a house! Yet attitudes towards child crime were changing. Whilst some argued that children should receive very harsh punishments – a 'short (or long), sharp, shock', as it was known – others were beginning to question the way society punished the young. Reformers like Mary Carpenter argued that locking up children with adult criminals was hardly likely to make them lead honest lives when they came out! And if a child had known nothing but crime from an early age, why should they be treated so harshly when they have never been taught the difference between right and wrong?

A step towards treating children differently came in 1838 when Parkhurst Prison was opened. It was the first designed solely for young people. However, conditions were incredibly hard. Youngsters spent the first four months of their sentence in silence on their own – then two years in leg irons!

In 1847, the Juvenile Offences Act said people under 16 should be tried in a special court, not an adult one. Seven years later, **reformatory schools** were set up in the hope that the tough conditions inside would 'persuade' children to give up their lives of crime. After spending two or three weeks inside an adult jail, children would be sent to reformatory schools to start their long sentence of hard labour, cold cells, a diet of bread and water and frequent beatings.

Now study the two sources very carefully. They are photographs of real children who committed real crimes and received real punishments. Their records are today kept in the Public Record Office in London.

Source A ▸ *The prison record of Elizabeth Roberts, aged 15.*

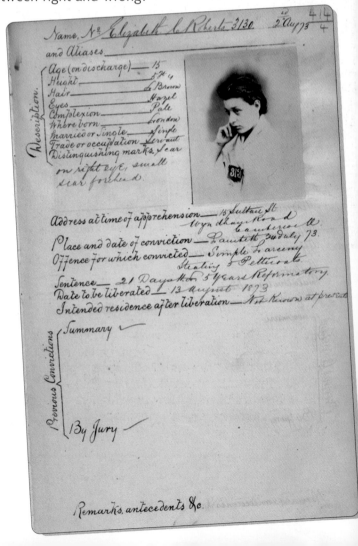

Source B ▾ *The prison record of George Page, aged 12. He doesn't look too happy, does he?*

Name. No. George Page 6402 16 Aug 73
and Aliases.
Age (on discharge) 12
Height 4 ft 3½ in
Hair Brown
Eyes Blue
Complexion Fresh
Where born Surrey
Married or Single Single
Trade or occupation None
Distinguishing marks Scar on forehead

Address at time of apprehension Abbs Court West Moulsey
Place and date of conviction Kingston 31 July 1873
Offence for which convicted Vagrant Wandering abroad having no visible means of subsistence.
Sentence 1 Cal Month H.L. 5 Years Reformatory.
Date to be liberated 30 August 1873
Intended residence after liberation Not Known at present

Summary
+ George Edney Page 24 April 73 Kingston
14 days * 4 years Reformatory
Simple Larceny Stg an axe 5/
J.O.A.

By Jury

Remarks, antecedents &c.
+ Return sent 26 April 73
* not sent to Reformatory.

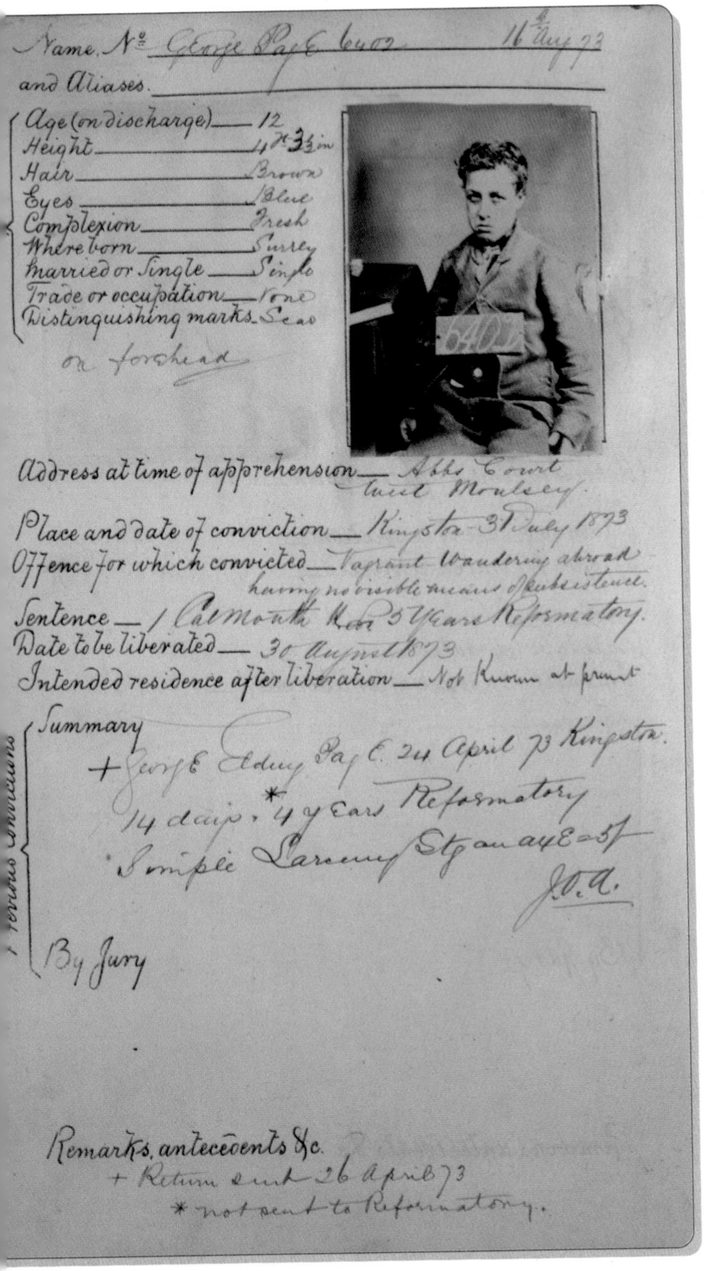

In 1870, the government decided that all children aged from five to ten would have to go to school. By 1900, every child under 12 went to school. It wasn't long before child crime figures began to drop – children were gaining a sense of right and wrong in school ... and they were no longer on the streets in the daytime getting into trouble!

From 1899 onwards, children were no longer sent to adult prisons for any part of their sentence. Instead, special new schools – called **borstals** – were set up to encourage young offenders to get involved in sport, healthy eating and learning new skills. Although still tough, staff weren't in uniform and young people were given a greater sense of responsibility.

WISE UP WORDS

- reformatory schools borstals

FACT *'Please sir, can I have some more?'*

Oliver Twist, the famous novel by Charles Dickens, was published in monthly instalments between 1837 and 1839. The account of a gang of young pickpockets, led by the Artful Dodger, played right into the hands of those people who were pushing for more and more severe punishments for young offenders!

WORK

1 Write a sentence or two about the following words or phrases: Parkhurst Prison • reformatory school • borstals

2 a Look at **Sources A** and **B** carefully, then complete a copy of the chart below.

NAME OF OFFENDER	AGE	OFFENCE COMMITTED	SENTENCE	ANY PREVIOUS CONVICTIONS? If so, give details
Elizabeth				
George				

b There are two parts to each sentence. Why do you think the Victorians: i) sent the offender to prison; ii) sent them on to reformatory school after?

c What do you think would happen to Elizabeth and George if they committed the same crimes today?

3 Imagine either Elizabeth or George escaped before their sentence was carried out. Design a wanted poster for one of them using the information in the source.

Who caught the vile Victorian villains?

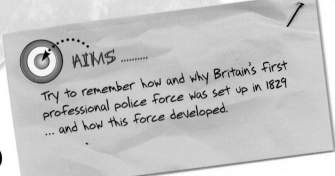

AIMS ....

Try to remember how and why Britain's first professional police force was set up in 1829 ... and how this force developed.

London had the worst crime problem because it was Britain's largest city. Naturally, it was the place where any new crime-fighting initiative would start. In 1750, a London magistrate named Henry Fielding decided to do something about the con men, beggars, thieves and prostitutes lurking around his offices in Bow Street. He gathered six men together, gave them each handcuffs, a pistol and a stick and promised to pay them a guinea (£1.05) a week to capture as many criminals as possible. At first, they wore their own clothes but were later given a uniform. This force of night-time thief takers became known as the Bow Street Runners (see **Source B**).

Source A ▾ *John Hopkins Warden, a constable in Bedford, talking about the problems of the old system of constables in 1821.*

"A part-time parish constable, who is new to the job every year, can't be aware of a criminal's plans and habits. He also has his own business to take care of. He knows that his time as a constable will soon end so he doesn't give the job the attention it requires."

staff (which could hold arrest warrant)

wore own clothes to begin with

handcuffs

pistol

Source B ▸ *A Bow Street Runner. Basically, they were constables who agreed to work for longer than the usual year.*

In 1763, Henry's blind brother, John, began a horse patrol to stop highwaymen on the roads leading in and out of London. It only lasted 18 months but a new patrol of 54 men was set up in 1805. A few years before that, in 1792, seven areas in London had set up their own police offices but London and the country as a whole needed far more. It needed a proper police force!

The man who played a major part in creating Britain's first professional police force was an MP named Sir Robert Peel. As part of his job as the government's Home Secretary, he was responsible for dealing with law and order. In 1829, he set up the Metropolitan Police Force to replace the Bow Street Runners.

Three thousand men, mainly ex-soldiers, were enlisted into a force and each given a new blue uniform, boots, a wooden truncheon, a rattle, a brown coat and a top hat lined with iron. They received 5p a day (not much then, but better than many other jobs) and were expected to walk their 20-mile 'beat' around London, seven days a week. They had to be less than 35 years of age, healthy and able to read and write. Discipline was severe and many early recruits were sacked for drunkenness. London, with its open sewers, dirty water and filthy air, was so unhealthy that many policemen died of tuberculosis or became unfit for duty!

To begin with, many hated the new police force. Some felt it was an invasion of privacy, a waste of money or a threat to an Englishman's freedom. Policemen were regularly beaten up in the street and spat at. Even early nicknames reflected the hostility towards them as they were branded 'Peel's bloody gang' and the 'evil blue devils'. But the 'blue devils' did a good job. They were well disciplined, good humoured and acted with restraint wherever possible (see **Source D**). Gradually, the public began to respect and trust them. More criminals were caught so there was less crime in London too! Soon other towns copied London's lead and, by 1856, every town in the country had its own policemen.

Source C ▾ *A policeman, 1829. These men soon became known as 'Peelers' or 'Bobbies' after the surname or Christian name of their founder.*

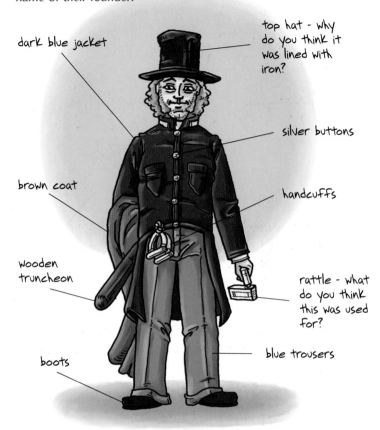

dark blue jacket

top hat - why do you think it was lined with iron?

silver buttons

brown coat

handcuffs

wooden truncheon

rattle - what do you think this was used for?

boots

blue trousers

Source D ▾ *Instructions given to policemen in 1829.*

"You must be polite and attentive to everyone. Rudeness will not be tolerated. You must act quickly and sensibly and have a perfect temper, never allowing yourself to be moved by any foul language or threats … police constables are asked not to pay any attention to any silly expressions which they may be called."

Source E ▾ *In 1810, the old system of watchmen and constables brought 9600 convictions. In 1830, there were 18 000 convictions for major crimes and by 1900, there were 25 000 convictions. The new police force seemed to be working.*

1830

3 000 policemen

1900

48 000 policemen

Source F ▾ *A photograph of some of Britain's first 'boys in blue'. They faced a tough life, working shifts seven days a week. Meal breaks didn't exist so food and drink was carried in a special blue bag and eaten 'on the beat'. Non-uniformed detectives, based at Scotland Yard, appeared in 1842 (after regular policemen messed up a murder hunt!) but policewomen didn't appear until the twentieth century.*

Source G ▾ *From an 1868 article in Fun Magazine, published shortly after riots in London. Mayne was the chief of police in London and it's clear his force weren't popular!*

"Richard Mayne is the leader of an organised gang of ruffians who annoy respectable people by playing at soldiers … the miscreants [evil-doers] wear helmets and commit other absurdities."

Source H ▾ *From* Punch *magazine, 1851. Six million tickets were sold for the exhibition at the Crystal Palace, London.*

"The police are beginning to take that place in the affections of the people – we don't mean the cooks and housemaids alone but the people at large – that the soldiers and sailors used to occupy. The blue coats – the defenders of order – are becoming the national favourites. The taking of a foreign fort seems to sink into insignificance before the taking of an unruly cabman's number. Everyone has been charmed during the Great Exhibition by the ways in which this truly Civil Power has been effective."

Source I ▾ *A cartoon from* Punch *magazine in October 1888.*

One criminal: 'Fine body of men the per-leece!'
Other: 'Uncommon fine – it's lucky for us there's so bloom'n few of 'em!'

FACT *Italian idiot?*

Detectives have always attempted to use the latest scientific techniques to catch criminals. In 1876, an Italian named Cesare Lombardo went a step further. He thought you could identify a criminal just by looking at them or feeling the bumps on their head! He studied over 7000 criminals and came up with his own guide to the criminal face!

Highwaymen — Odd shaped heads, thick hair, thick beards.

Muggers — Short, broad head, long hands.

Fire-bombers — Long arms and legs, small head, light weight.

Attackers of women — Short hands, medium-sized brains, narrow foreheads, thick light hair, odd shaped noses.

Assassins — Large jaw, thick black hair, thin beard, pale face.

WORK

1 Each of these dates is important in the history of the police:

   1829 • 1805 • 1750 • 1792 • 1763 • 1842 • 1856

   Write each date on a separate line, in chronological order. Beside each date, write what happened in that year.

2 **a** Was the idea of having a police force in London entirely new in 1829?

   b Why was the first official police force set up in 1829?

   c Explain why people were at first against having a regular police force.

   d How did the police try to 'win people over' and earn their respect?

3 Look at **Source C**. Why do you think the policemen were equipped with: i) a rattle; ii) a truncheon; iii) a hat lined with iron?

4 Look at **Source I**. Is this source for or against the police? Think very carefully about your answer.

The end of the Bloody Code

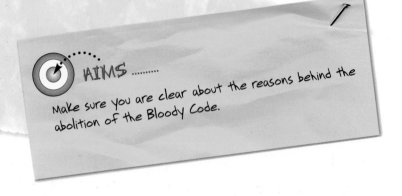

AIMS ....

Make sure you are clear about the reasons behind the abolition of the Bloody Code.

Since the early 1700s, the number of crimes punishable by death had gone up and up. Governments had responded to rising lawlessness and the public's fear of crime by making punishments increasingly savage.

By the 1820s, there were nearly 200 hanging crimes, including shooting a rabbit, stealing a sheep, scribbling on Westminster Bridge or digging up a tree in Downing Street! The whole criminal justice system, with its focus on secure punishments, became known as the 'Bloody Code'. But did the Bloody Code actually work? Did it increase the number of executions? And why, eventually, was the Bloody Code **abolished**?

Since the introduction of the Bloody Code, a bitter battle had waged over the offences for which a person could be executed (see **Source A**).

Source A ▼ *Two common, opposing views of the Bloody Code.*

'The fear of death is the best way to frighten people into behaving. As many crimes as possible should be punishable by execution. Perhaps we don't need to hang everyone who commits a capital crime - but just enough to make people think twice about breaking the law. And yes, we may hang a few innocent men now and again but their death is for the good of everyone!'

'Public hangings don't scare anyone. You only have to go to one to see how people actually enjoy the occasion. All that laughing and joking whilst someone gets their neck stretched - they're hardly frightened; entertained more like! Harsh punishments don't deter people from a career in crime because they know they're not likely to get caught. A better deterrent would be a better policing system and a greater chance of arrest. More money into policing and a better prison system is what's needed!'

Source B ▾ *MP Sir William Meredith, complaining to Parliament about the Bloody Code in 1770.*

"A man who has stolen something worth thirty pence is punished with the same severity as if he had murdered a whole family. None should be punished with death except in cases of murder."

FACT *Hangings*

In 1785, 97 people were executed in England. Only one of these was hanged for murder; the other 96 were hanged for theft!

The effectiveness of the Bloody Code

By the early 1800s, it was becoming clear to many people in government that the attempt to reduce crime through the use of the Bloody Code wasn't working. Witnesses, judges and juries often took pity on criminals, especially young children, and said they were not guilty rather than have them hanged. Witnesses would swear goods taken by a prisoner were worth four shillings, not five, and so save them from the gallows. And many sentences of death were never actually carried out – over half those sentenced to death between 1761 and 1765 had their sentences reduced to transportation. Worse still, one chilling result of the Bloody Code was that some thieves, faced with the prospect of being hung for theft, actually murdered their victims to reduce the chance of being identified as the attacker. After all, the punishment was the same!

A campaign to abolish the death penalty for many trivial crimes was started in Parliament by James Mackintosh and Sir Samuel Romilly. In 1808, Romilly got a law passed abolishing the death sentence for pickpocketing. By the 1820s, Sir Robert Peel, the government's Home Secretary (responsible for law and order) successfully began to argue in Parliament that savage punishment was not the answer to crime. He said that it was much better to catch more criminals with an efficient police force and punish them in decent jails than let 99 out of every 100 escape and punish the hundredth by execution.

Between 1822 and 1840, Peel reduced the number of crimes for which a person could be hanged from over 200 to about five. The changes were bitterly opposed by some in Parliament, who said the 'softer' treatment of criminals would just increase crime. After 1841, the only crimes for which hanging remained were murder, treason, piracy with violence and burning down a weapons store or a dockyard. Despite lots of opposition to the changes, like Peel forecast, the crime rate did not increase. Public hanging ended in 1868 – the Bloody Code was dead!

Source C ▾ *The number of executions in Cheshire, 1580–1710.*

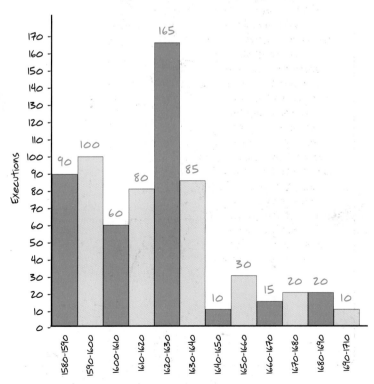

Source D ▲ *Sir Robert Peel. Peel worked for up to 16 hours a day and was a brilliant speaker. He realised that if Britain were to avoid the revolutions that had swept Europe in the mid-1800s, there would have to be big changes made in Britain. He was Prime Minister twice and died in 1850 after falling off his horse.*

Source E ▼ *These figures show the numbers of people hanged in London and Devon per year within two time periods. It seems that fewer people were hanged under the Bloody Code than before it.*

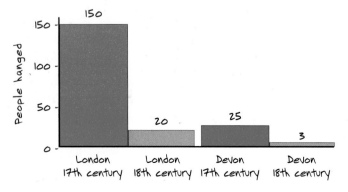

Source F ▼ *A graph showing crime figures, 1750–1900.*

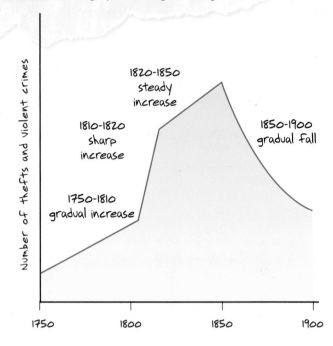

Most historians believe the graph in **Source F** is fairly accurate. The falling crime rate after 1850 can be explained because:

- Prisons were no longer 'schools for crime'. Instead, attempts were made to reform the prisoners.
- The system of punishment was a lot fairer. Criminals were not 'let off' a crime because the jury didn't want to give them a death sentence. At the same time, criminals who were caught received adequate punishments.
- A police force operated which deterred some criminals from committing crimes.

Obviously, an explanation of a falling crime rate isn't that simple. It's not enough to say that crime fell because of police, prisons and a new code of punishment. The period 1850–1900 was one of more prosperity and as you are aware, crime falls when people have jobs, food and some money in their pockets … and increases when they are poor (note that the time between 1810 and 1820 was one of food shortages and poverty!). However, it *is* clear that the two factors – better policing, prison and punishments *and* a more prosperous Britain – worked together to reduce crime.

WISE UP WORD

- abolish

Source G ▾ *A simple explanation of the changes and effects of new policing, prisons and punishments between 1750 and 1900.*

1800s

Overcrowded prisons

Night watchmen and constables

Many offences led to execution

= more crime

1900s

Improved prison conditions

Peel's police force

Execution for fewer crimes, for example, murder and treason

= less crime

WORK

1 Look at **Source A**.

   a Briefly write down what you understand by the term 'Bloody Code'.

   b In your own words, summarise the main arguments for and against the 'Bloody Code'.

2 Look at **Source C**.

   a In the 1680s, there were about 50 crimes punishable by death. By the early 1700s, there were over 100. What does this source tell us about the number of executions during this period?

   b Can you explain why there were fewer people executed than should have been?

3 Imagine you are one of the many MPs in the 1820s who were against the Bloody Code. They wanted it abolished. Based on the points below, write a five-minute speech that could be given to Parliament.

   • The Bloody Code isn't working – serious crimes are still committed.
   • Juries don't give death sentences anyway.
   • We should use alternatives, like transportation.
   • Let's be forward thinking and try to change the criminal rather than kill them.
   • Let's have a better police force in order to deter crime through the fear of being caught.

   Start your speech 'My honourable gentlemen, as you know, I am dead against the Bloody Code...'

SUMMARY

• A professional police force was introduced in London in 1829. By 1856, forces had been set up nationwide.

• There was a wide range of laws, including many new ones. As the government became more and more involved in all aspects of society, they introduced laws to encourage people to conform. For example, it became a criminal offence for a factory owner to work children too hard in their mills.

• The Bloody Code was abolished and, by 1900, the only crimes punishable by death were murder and treason. The system of trials did not change very much.

• Punishments no longer took place in public (the last public hanging was in 1868) and prisons became the main form of punishment. The aim was to punish and reform the prisoner rather than warn others against committing crimes. Transportation was used until 1868 as a 'middle' way between executing the criminal and fining them.

Case study: Why was Jack the Ripper never caught?

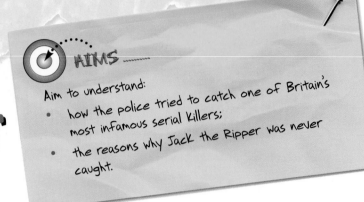

AIMS

Aim to understand:
- how the police tried to catch one of Britain's most infamous serial killers;
- the reasons why Jack the Ripper was never caught.

It had been an unusually cold day in London on Thursday 30 August 1888. At 11:00pm, prostitute Mary Ann Nichols, sometimes known as Polly, was seen shivering outside The Frying Pan pub in Whitechapel, a notoriously dangerous area of London. She was looking for customers. Just after midnight, she returned to the room she had been sharing with other prostitutes. At about 1:30am, her landlord threw her out of her bedsit because she was behind with her rent. As she walked away, someone heard her shout, 'save me my bed, I'll soon get your money'. At about 2:30am, one of Mary Ann's pals saw her back outside the pub. She was described as 'very drunk and staggering against walls'. Mary Ann told her friend, Emily Holland, that she had earned her rent money three times over but had spent it on booze. She said she was going to look for one more customer, then return to the bedsit to pay her landlord.

At 4:00am, Mary Ann was found murdered. Her throat had been slashed with a long-bladed knife and her stomach had been cut open. Just over a week later, another prostitute called Annie Chapman – or 'Dark Annie' – was found dead in a backyard only a few hundred metres from the first murder. A doctor called to the scene wrote that 'the body was terribly mutilated and the throat deeply severed.' The killer had removed some of Annie's internal organs too and placed them over her shoulder. Other body parts were also missing.

It didn't take police long to realise they had a violent serial killer on their hands. Then, on 27 September, a London newspaper received an amazing letter (see **Source B**). The writer boasted of the killings and teased the police for not catching him. Within days, gruesome details of the murders appeared in newspapers all over Britain. The press didn't care whether the letter was from the genuine killer or not, they just knew that descriptions of crimes sold newspapers – and they were happy to print all the details they could. They even began using the name that the writer of the first letter had given himself – Jack the Ripper!

So why is Jack the Ripper so famous? How many women did he kill? Who were the main suspects? How did the police try to track him down? Was he ever caught? And what does the Jack the Ripper story tell us about crime and policing in the late nineteenth century?

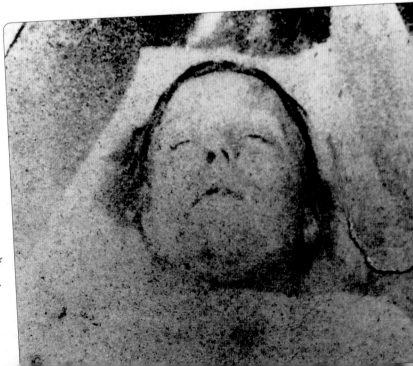

Source A ▶ *A photograph of the corpse of Mary Ann Nichols.*

Pause for thought

- The police immediately thought the killer might be a butcher or a doctor – why?

- In the 'Dear Boss' letter, what do you think is the 'red stuff' he was writing about?

- Do you think the letter gives police any clues about the writer's education, ethnic background or sex?

Source B ▶ *This is a transcript of a letter received by the press on 27 September. It is known as the 'Dear Boss' letter. Specialists think this could have been sent by the real killer although they can't ever be 100% sure. Note: The 'Leather Apron' mentioned in the letter refers to a man of this nickname who police arrested and later released because he had an alibi on the night of each murder. You should also be aware that all spelling mistakes, underlining and grammar have been left the same as the original letter. An image of the real letter appears below.*

"Dear Boss,

I keep on hearing the police have caught me but they wont fix me just yet. I have laughed when they look so clever and talk about being on the <u>right</u> track. That joke about Leather Apron gave me real fits. I am down on whores and I shant quit ripping them till I do get buckled. Grand work the last job was. I gave the lady no time to squeal. How can they catch me now. I love my work and want to start again. You will soon hear of me with my funny little games. I saved some of the proper <u>red</u> stuff in a ginger beer bottle over the last job to write with but it went thick like glue and I cant use it. Red ink is fit enough I hope <u>ha</u>. <u>ha</u>. The next job I do I shall clip the ladys ears off and send to the police officers just for jolly wouldn't you. Keep this letter back till I do a bit more work, then give it out straight. My knife's so nice and sharp I want to get to work right away if I get a chance. Good Luck.

Yours truly

Jack the Ripper

Dont mind me giving the trade name

PS Wasnt good enough to post this before I got all the red ink off my hands curse it No luck yet. They say I'm a doctor now. <u>ha ha</u>"

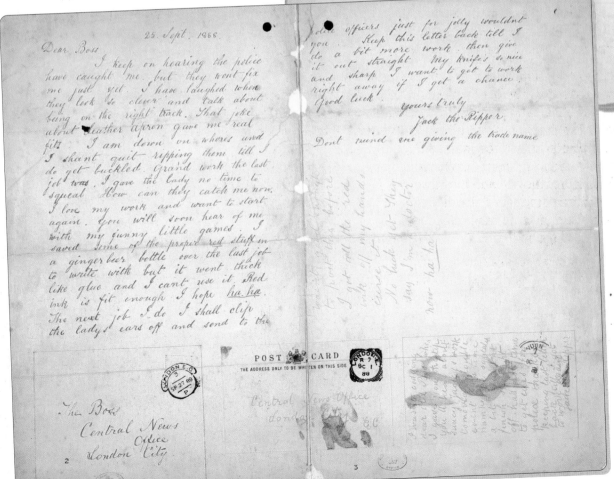

Source C ▼ *A photograph of the backyard of 29 Hanbury Street, Whitechapel. 'Dark Annie' Chapman's body was dumped here.*

Source D ▼ *A mortuary photograph of Elizabeth Stride.*

Source E ▼ *An illustration that appeared in a London newspaper showing the police discovery of the body of Catherine Eddowes.*

More murders

On 30 September, two more prostitutes were murdered … on the same night! 'Long Liz' Stride was found in a yard off Berner Street at 1:00am. Her throat had been cut. Later, police concluded that the killer must have been disturbed before she could be mutilated. In fact, the man who found her and raised the alarm said her body was still warm when he first touched her – and his horse was behaving oddly, as if someone was hiding nearby! An hour later, the body of Catherine Eddowes was discovered. Police found graffiti near her body that read, 'The Juwes are the men that will not be blamed for nothing'. However, it was washed off, fearing attacks on Jews living in the Whitechapel area whom English residents already thought might be responsible for the attacks. Next to the graffiti were bits of Catherine's blood-soaked apron that the killer had used to wipe his knife. Later, doctors found that one of her ears, her nose and some of her kidney had been removed!

On the morning of 1 October, another letter arrived at the headquarters of a London news office. The letter makes reference to the 'double event' of the night before and bears a remarkable resemblance to the 'Dear Boss' letter. Expert analysis shows that the handwriting is similar in both letters (see **Source F**).

Source F ▾ *This letter was sent to the Central News Agency, a London press office, on 1 October 1888. Note that the writer remarks 'thanks for keeping the last letter back'. This refers to the fact that newspapers didn't print the first 'Dear Boss' letter until early on the morning of 1 October. Those who believe this letter to be written by the real Ripper argue that the letter carries accurate details of the 'double event' killing of Stride and Eddowes before all the details appeared in the newspapers.*

> *I was not codding dear old Boss when I gave you the tip, you'll hear about Saucy Jacky's work tomorrow double event this time number one squealed a bit couldn't finish straight off. ha not the time to get ears off for police.*
>
> Jack the Ripper

Pause for thought

Why do you think many people believe the second letter (**Source F**) was written by the same person as the first letter (**Source B**)?

Then, on 16 October, a Mr George Lusk, president of a new neighbourhood group based in Whitechapel, received a gruesome delivery through the post. Inside a small box was half a kidney preserved in wine, together with yet another letter (see **Source G**).

Source G ▾ *The 'From hell' letter. Police were unable to tell for sure if the letter came from the same person as the first two letters. However, most detectives felt different people wrote them. Dr Openshaw, the man asked to examine the kidney, thought it looked very similar to the one removed from Catherine Eddowes (although he couldn't be sure!).*

> *From hell*
> *Mr Lusk Sor,*
>
> *I send you half the Kidne I took from one woman and prasarved it for you tother piece I fried and ate it was very nise. I may send you the bloody Knife that took it out if you only wate a whil longer*
>
> *Signed*
> *Catch me when you can Mishter Lusk*

Pause for thought

Do you think the third letter is from the killer? Give reasons for your answer.

On 9 November, a fifth prostitute was murdered. Her rent collector found Mary Kelly's body inside the room she rented. She was the only Ripper victim to be found indoors and the only one to be photographed at the scene by police (see **Source H**). Police found Mary's clothes neatly folded on a chair and her books in front of the fire. She had been cut open, her organs placed around the room and her face hacked to pieces.

Source H ▾ *The mutilated body of Mary Kelly, the Ripper's last known victim.*

By mid-November, news of the killings had spread all over the world. Stories appeared in 160 newspapers as far away as Australia and Mexico. A Polish newspaper told its readers of the 'Panic in London', whilst a Jamaican one described 'Whitechapel's Brutal Murders'.

So how many did he kill ... exactly?

It is unclear just how many women Jack the Ripper killed. It is generally accepted that he killed five women – Nichols, Chapman, Stride, Eddowes and Kelly – but some experts think he killed even more. Even the public, newspapers and some policemen at the time thought he might be responsible for as many as 13 deaths. However, the detectives in charge of the case decided to keep the figure at five.

> **Pause for thought**
>
> Why do you think police at the time decided to keep the Ripper's murder record at five?

Source I ▼ *From a modern history textbook.*

"Whitechapel in 1888 was a sink of poverty and crime. Of the 76 000 inhabitants, 40% lived below the poverty line. Around 8500 people slept in one of the 233 lodging houses. Half the population were poor Jewish immigrants, but Irish, Russians, Poles and many other races lived there. There were (at least) 1200 prostitutes. The Victorians believed that soldiers needed prostitutes and the Contagious Diseases Act gave police the right to arrest and brutally examine prostitutes to make sure they were 'clean'."

Where did Jack strike?

London, in 1888, was a divided city. The West End of the city was home to wealthier Londoners whilst the East End was crowded with the slum housing of the poor. Jack the Ripper operated in the East End, in the so-called 'evil square mile', which included the districts of Whitechapel, Spitalfields and Aldgate. In fact, the East End was the ideal environment for crime. Smoke and stinking gases from factories and housing choked the narrow city streets so badly that, at times, it wasn't possible to see more than a metre in front of your face. Dark passages and alleyways provided excellent cover for any thief, mugger ... or murderer!

Source J ▼ *A map of the Whitechapel area of London's East End showing where each victim was found. The maze-like streets were full of pubs, houses for rent and cheap 'doss houses' where people could buy a bed in a room for a few pennies per week. As there was no 'dole' money for any women without work, many were forced to become prostitutes to survive. Many became helpless alcoholics to escape their terrible lives. It was these women who were the Ripper's prey!*

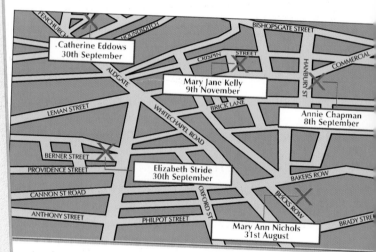

How did Jack kill?

A few years ago, experts put together a detailed report of the way Jack the Ripper killed his victims. Using photographs, sketches, police reports and doctors' notes made at the time, they were able to gain a good understanding of the Ripper's **modus operandi** (see **Source K**).

Source K ▼ *The way Jack the Ripper killed was only established recently.*

MODUS OPERANDI

Killer: Jack the Ripper, AKA The Whitechapel Murderer

Victim(s): Five Whitechapel prostitutes

Date(s): August–November, 1888

Location: Whitechapel, Spitalfields, Aldgate, City of London

Method: He strangled his victims until they were dead or unconscious.

Evidence: Doctors concluded that all victims had been strangled at some point in the attack.

Method: He lowered his victims gently to the floor.

Evidence: There is no bruising on the back of any victims' heads to indicate that they had been thrown onto the floor.

Method: Throats were slashed whilst the women were on the ground.

Evidence: There were no bloodstains down the front of any victims' dresses – there would have been if they had been cut whilst standing up. Also, at the scene, the blood pooled beside or under the neck, indicating that the victims were lying down with their head to the side when they were cut.

Method: The Ripper was probably left-handed.

Evidence: Cut marks on each victim show that he straddled over the body at or near the feet and made his mutilations from the victim's right side. This indicates that the Ripper held his long-bladed knife in his left hand.

Notes: The Ripper must have had some experience of using a knife and/or medical knowledge. Due to the fact that he must have had to kill quickly, he managed to remove body parts and internal organs expertly. In one case (Catherine Eddowes), he removed a kidney from the front, rather than from the side and managed not to damage any of the surrounding organs.

Were there any witnesses?

Name of witness	Near to which scene was the Ripper seen?	Time of sighting	What did the Ripper look like?
Emily Walter	Annie Chapman	2:00am	Foreigner aged 37, dark beard and moustache. Wearing short dark jacket, dark vest and trousers, black scarf and black felt hat.
Elizabeth Long	Annie Chapman	5:30am	Dark complexion, brown deerstalker hat, possibly a dark overcoat. Aged over 40, somewhat taller than Chapman. A foreigner.
J Best and John Gardner	Elizabeth Stride	11:00pm	5'5" tall, English, black moustache, blond eyelashes, weak, wearing a suit and a hat.
William Marchall	Elizabeth Stride	11:45pm	Small, black coat, dark trousers, middle aged, round cap with a small sailor-like peak. 5'6", stout, appearance of a clerk. No moustache, no gloves, with a coat.
Matthew Packer	Elizabeth Stride	12:00–12:30pm	Aged 25–30, clean-shaven and respectable appearance, 5'7", hard, dark, felt deerstalker hat, dark clothes. Carrying a newspaper parcel 18 x 7 inches.
James Brown	Elizabeth Stride	12:45am	5'7", stout, long black coat which reached almost to his heels.
Israel Schwartz	Elizabeth Stride	12:45am	**First man**: Aged 30, 5'5", brown haired, fair complexion, small brown moustache, full face, broad shoulders, dark jacket and trousers, black cap with peak.
			Second man: Aged 35, 5'11", fresh complexion, light brown hair, dark overcoat, old, black, hard felt hat with a wide brim, clay pipe.
Joseph Lawende	Catherine Eddowes	1:30am	Aged 30, 5'7", fair complexion, brown moustache, coat, red neckerchief, grey peaked cloth cap. Sailor-like.
James Blenkinsop	Catherine Eddowes	1:30am	Well-dressed.
Mary Ann Cox	Mary Kelly	11:45pm	Short, stout man, shabbily dressed. Hat, blotchy face, carroty moustache, holding can of beer.
George Hutchinson	Mary Kelly	2:00am	Aged 34–35, 5'6", pale complexion, dark hair, slight moustache curled at each end, long dark coat, dark jacket underneath. Light waistcoat, thick gold chain with a red stone seal, dark trousers and button boots, gaiters, white buttons. White shirt; black tie fastened with a horseshoe pin. Dark hat turned down in middle. Red handkerchief. Jewish and respectable in appearance.

Source L ▲ *A summary of each of the main witness statements. As you can see from the variety of descriptions, the job of narrowing down the search by working out what the Ripper looked like was very difficult.*

The police interviewed over 2000 people, including any witnesses who had claimed to have seen some of the victims with 'mysterious looking' men shortly before their murder. However, all witnesses gave slightly different descriptions and police were never able to narrow down their search to men of a certain height, weight, hair colour, class or ethnic background. They were not able to put together an 'artist's impression' of the killer either.

So what did the police do?

The police worked hard to track down the killer using all methods available to them at the time. Despite being heavily criticised, especially by newspapers, the police explored many interesting avenues of investigation.

- Over 2000 people were interviewed. Police talked to sailors from the docks, drug addicts, lodgers, prostitutes, gypsies, doctors and even American visitors from a travelling 'wild west' show. Seventy-six butchers and slaughterers were interrogated about their work and colleagues.

- Police handed out over 80 000 leaflets and posters appealing for information and witnesses.

- Police trained a group of bloodhounds to 'sniff out' any leads. The dogs were taken out to each murder scene but failed to pick up on the killer's scent. After all, on the dark and smelly streets of Whitechapel, it was highly unlikely that a dog would manage to follow any single scent. At the end of October, the experiment was abandoned.

- Male policemen (there were no women police officers in 1888) even dressed up in women's clothes and posed as prostitutes to see if the killer approached them (see **Source M**). After a few outings, the police abandoned this idea too.

Source M ▼ *This letter was sent to police chiefs by a member of the public. They tried his idea – without success!*

How to catch the killer

11 November 1888

Urgent plan for trapping the Whitechapel Murderer

Let a number of men, say 12, be selected, of short stature, and as far as possible of effeminate [looking like a woman] appearance, but of known courage and tried nerve.

Dress them as females of the class from whom the victims are selected, arm them with the best and lightest weapons and distribute them over the district haunted by the murderer.

Note: the men would require to be fair actors … and the whole scheme would have to be absolutely secret, for once the press get a hint of it, any chance of success will be gone.

Thomas Blair, Dumfries

Despite tracking down every good lead and interrogating every suspect thoroughly, the police were no nearer to catching the murderer by the end of 1888 than they had been after the death of the first victim. The police were ridiculed in newspapers and magazines (see **Source N**) and even Queen Victoria was furious. She remarked, 'These new, most ghastly murders show the necessity for some very decided action. All the courts [enclosed yards] must be lit and our detectives improved. They are not what they should be.'

Source N ▼ *A cartoon from Punch magazine, September 1888. It is called 'Blind Man's Buff'.*

Pause for thought

What does this cartoon suggest about the police?

Why was 'Jack' never caught?

In November 1888, the killings suddenly stopped. Although police identified many suspects, no one was ever charged with the Ripper murders. To this day, the killer's identity remains a mystery. So how did Jack the Ripper get away with such brutal – and high profile – crimes?

• Poor witnesses

All the people who claimed to have seen the victims talking to a man who may have been the Ripper gave a different description. This meant that a police sketch artist could never create an 'artist's impression' for the police to use on the streets of Whitechapel.

Was it black or brown hair?

• The letters

London's newspapers received hundreds of letters from people who claimed to be the killer. Most of them were obvious fakes so the press didn't take any of them very seriously at all. However, experts today believe that at least one of the letters (**Source B** – the 'Dear Boss' letter) was from the **real** Ripper. Yet the press didn't give it to the police straightaway, thinking it was another fake. The night after the police finally received the letter (which promises to kill more women 'right away'), Elizabeth Stride and Catherine Eddowes were murdered. Did the delay in giving the letter to police cost these two women their lives? Could the police have put out even more undercover patrols if they knew the Ripper was going to strike straight away?

• Newspaper interference

Despite the horrific nature of the Ripper's crimes, editors were pleased to fill their newspapers with gruesome descriptions of each killing. They knew that crime reports sold newspapers – especially serial murders with a sexual element! And every time the press reported a fresh murder, often by writing about as much blood and guts as they could, the middle and upper classes living in the wealthier parts of London complained to their politicians. This resulted in the government putting pressure on the police force to solve the case quickly. Experienced police officers working on the case were constantly transferred to other cases. The constant changing within the police force, as a result of the panic created by the press, made progress on the Ripper case very slow.

• Lack of a reward

A reward for information leading to the arrest of the murderer was never offered despite police offering rewards for information about *other* serious crimes.

• No forensic evidence

Forensic science is the scientific study of objects involved in a crime. Today, this includes fingerprint analysis and DNA comparison. At the time of the Whitechapel murders, the only way to prove someone had committed a murder was to catch them doing it, or get a suspect to confess. Forensic evidence was not available to them so taking witness statements and examining dead bodies was all they knew how to do. In fact, in 1888, police still believed that taking a photograph of the victim's eyes shortly after death would show the image of the murderer imprinted on their eyeballs.

• Police problems

The sites of the Ripper murders crossed the area where two separate police forces patrolled. As a result, both the Metropolitan Police Force *and* the City of London Police Force committed officers to the investigation. Perhaps you might think that this would have helped to catch the killer. It didn't! Although the policemen from each force worked well together out on the streets, the men in charge of the two forces didn't cooperate too well at all. Not all information was shared and there are suggestions of rivalry between the force commanders. Unfortunately, this led to policemen wasting their time looking for information that the other force already knew.

GHASTLY MURDER IN THE EAST END

Dreadful Mutilation of a Woman

Another murder even more diabolical than the last ... the woman's body had been completely slashed open and her heart and other pieces lay about the place ... portions of the entrails lay round the victim's neck. An excited crowd gathered...

Source O ◄ *Part of a front-page report of a large London newspaper, September 1888.*

Who were the suspects?

A few years after the last of the murders, the man in charge of policing in Britain named his three top suspects. They were:

- **M J Druitt** – a lawyer and teacher who had trained as a doctor. Even his own family thought he might be the 'Ripper'. He killed himself in December 1888.

- **Aaron Kosminiski** – a lunatic who heard voices and would only eat from the gutter. Police who worked for a long time on the case thought it could be him.

- **Michael Ostrogg** – a Russian doctor who worked in a women's hospital. He went back to Russia shortly after the last murder and was eventually sent to a mental hospital for stabbing a woman in St Petersburg.

Other popular Ripper suspects include an artist named Walter Sickert, a cotton merchant named James Maybrick, an American doctor named Francis Tumblety and a barber called George Chapman who was convicted of poisoning two of his wives. He lived in Whitechapel at the time of the murders and trained as a doctor! Over the years, many writers and historians have claimed to know who the real Ripper was ... but no one has ever proved anything!

> **FACT** A 2001 film *From Hell* charts the Ripper murders and proposes Queen Victoria's grandson – Prince Albert Victor – as the main suspect. In total, there have been at least 12 Ripper movies, four TV series and over 200 books. Experts on the subject are even known as Ripperologists!

WISE UP WORD

- modus operandi

WORK

1. The following eight events have all been mixed up. Put them in the correct chronological order.
   - Murder of Elizabeth Stride
   - Second 'Dear Boss' letter arrives
   - Murder of Mary Kelly
   - Murder of Mary Ann Nichols
   - George Lusk receives letter and human body parts through post
   - Murder of Annie Chapman
   - Murder of Catherine Eddowes
   - First 'Dear Boss' letter arrives

2. **a** What problems did the police have during the Ripper investigation? Make a list of them.
   b Which of these problems do you consider most important and why?

3. Look at **Source N**. What does this cartoon suggest about attitudes to the police during the Ripper investigation?

4. **a** What is meant by the term 'modus operandi'?
   b In your own words, explain Jack's modus operandi.
   c Can you think of any reasons why Jack chose the Whitechapel area of London to hunt for victims?

5. Why do you think the Whitechapel murders attracted so much attention?

6. Look at **Source L**. Using the witness statements, design a 'WANTED' poster for 'Jack the Ripper'.
   - Draw a full-length 'artist's impression'.
   - Include a BEWARE file warning the public what to watch out for: physical appearance, usual clothing, approximate age, 'killing time', favourite 'haunts' and any other useful information.

   TOP TIP: Make sure you do a draft copy, then a neat one on A3 paper – it will make a great class display.

Why were protesters treated so harshly between 1700 and 1850?

AIMS ....

Ensure you understand:
• Why different groups protested between 1700 and 1850;
• how the government reacted and why they reacted in the way they did.

Governments have never been able to please all of the people all of the time. When large numbers of people are unhappy about something, they tend to join together to protest. Sometimes these protests are peaceful. At other times, they turn violent. These more violent protests are usually called riots.

Pause for thought

• Can you think of any issues in recent years, locally or nationally, over which large numbers of people have gathered together to protest?

• Have you ever protested against anything by gathering with others in a large group?

In 1715, the Riot Act was introduced (see **Source A**). King George I had wanted it because he feared a rebellion. Soon it was being used to break up all sorts of protest meetings. In fact, almost any meeting that the government wanted to stop was called a riot … and there were hundreds of them! Riots against new taxes, wars, food prices, new roads, new machinery, elections, religion – even riots over the introduction of a new calendar!

Source A ▼ Some rules of the Riot Act of 1715. You may have heard of the phrase, 'I'll have to go and read them the Riot Act'! It originates from this piece of legislation.

The Riot Act, 1715

• It is a hanging offence for 12 or more people to meet together and then not disperse (go home) if a magistrate tells them to!

• A magistrate may call in the soldiers to break up the crowd.

By order of Parliament

Source B ▼ American visitor, Benjamin Franklin, 1769.

"I have seen within a year, riots in the country about corn; riots about elections; riots about workhouses; riots of coal workers; riots of weavers; riots of political reformers; riots of smugglers in which custom house officers have been murdered and the King's armed ships and troops fired at."

So why was the government so worried about protesters?

In the eighteenth century, the people in power were mostly rich landowners from the upper class. They saw every protest as the beginning of a revolution that would sweep them out of power. The following cartoons sum up the fears of much of the landowning class in the early 1800s.

'What is the working class trying to prove? We provide them with their work and money, which puts food on their tables. If they remove us from power, destroy our machinery, block our roads and refuse to pay our taxes, it will be them who suffer in the end. We must be tough with them for their sakes!'

'The French Revolution of 1789 has worried me a lot! Poor, starving people removed King Louis from the throne and beheaded him – and much of the upper class with all the power lost their heads too! We must be tough with any protest.'

'All these riots and protests are no good for this country. They disrupt work and trade and damage the whole country in general. Calling in soldiers to deal with these riots is the patriotic thing to do!'

Between 1790 and 1850, there were over 700 protests in Britain, many of which turned to full-scale riots. They took place in both towns and the countryside in many parts of Britain. Over the next six pages, you will briefly study five different protests.

Many of the protesters were hanged whilst others were transported to Australia. Whilst studying each protest, try to think about:

- the reasons for the protest;
- the method of protest;
- how the authorities reacted and why they reacted in that way;
- how the protesters were punished.

The Luddites

In the early 1800s, new machinery in factories was making lots more cloth at cheaper prices than knitters and weavers could in their own homes. They just couldn't compete against a machine that could work all day and all night! Men and women who had earned just enough to get by for many years found their wages falling – and just at a time when food prices were rising. So the knitters and weavers fought back!

In 1811, organised gangs smashed about 1000 new machines in Nottingham and Derbyshire. The gang members were called **Luddites** after their leader, Ned Ludd, who lived secretly in Sherwood Forest. (Ludd was probably a mythical figure – if he really lived, no one found him!)

By 1812, the violence had spread to Yorkshire and Lancashire. The gangs struck at night under cover of darkness and, with no proper police force at the time, the Luddites seemed unstoppable.

But the government struck back. Britain was at war with France at the time and politicians felt that they couldn't fight a war *and* deal with riots at home. After a huge gunfight involving government soldiers and 150 Luddites outside William Cartwright's mill near Huddersfield in June 1812, 'machine breaking' became a hanging offence. In 1813, 14 of the Luddites who had attacked Cartwright's mill were hanged ... and the harsh punishments seemed to work. The riots became fewer after 1813 and this, coupled with cheaper food and slightly higher wages, saw an end to the protest movement of Ned Ludd and his Luddites.

Source C ▾ *A Luddite attack on machinery in a textile factory. The workers thought the machines would take away their jobs.*

Source D ▾ *Adapted from a letter sent by 'Ned Ludd' to Mr Smith, a factory owner in Yorkshire, 1812.*

" Dear Sir,

Information has just been given to me that you own some of those detestable shearing-frame machines and I was asked by men to write to you and give you fair warning to pull them down. If they are not taken down by the end of the week, I shall send at least 300 men to destroy them.

Ned Ludd "

FACT *No way for a lady to behave*

In 1839, in Wales, a group of farmers dressed up in women's clothes and tore down the new toll gates that had recently been installed near their farms. They were furious at the high tolls on the new roads. The government sent nearly 2000 soldiers and seventy policemen to calm the area – and even offered a £500 reward for the capture of riot leaders. A few leaders were caught and five sentenced to transportation. Eventually, the area calmed down after the government took over all the new toll roads. However, the mythical main leader – a woman called Rebecca – was never captured! These were known as the Rebecca Riots.

Peterloo

In the 1800s, only a small number of men (rich ones) had been allowed to vote or hold any position of power in government. This had been the same for hundreds of years. Many ordinary people thought this was unfair. They believed that politicians would listen more closely to their complaints about their lives if they were voters. On 16 August 1819, a huge meeting was held in St Peter's Field, Manchester. Sixty thousand men, women and children attended to hear famous speakers like Henry Hunt talk about the right of people to vote. Many held banners demanding 'Votes for all' and 'Freedom and peace'. But events got out of hand and the meeting became one of the most famous events of the nineteenth century – the 'Peterloo Massacre'.

Soon after the meeting began, local magistrates, who were worried about the size of the crowd, sent in armed soldiers to arrest the main speaker, Henry Hunt. The soldiers were shouted at and hustled by the crowd so the magistrates ordered in the cavalry, elite horsemen carrying razor-sharp swords, to charge at the crowd. In less than an hour, 11 people lay dead and 400 more were injured. The youngest victim was a baby, William Fildes, who was knocked out of his mother's arms and trampled to death by horses.

The whole event caused great anger and many demanded that the magistrates were punished. In fact, the government thanked the magistrates and Henry Hunt was jailed for two years. Parliament, worried about revolution, sent troops to areas of the country where they feared rebellion and rushed through six new Acts of Parliament (see **Source F**). Although the six acts were only in place for a year (protests dropped for a while after 1820 when lower food prices and more work reduced the demand for change), it was clear that the government's main objective at the start of the 1800s was to stop rebellion at any cost rather than listen to the public's complaints about poverty, unemployment and their rights.

> *Pause for thought*
>
> • What is the artist's attitude to the events at Peterloo?
>
> • In what way is the artist's attitude likely to affect their drawing?

Source E ▶ *A cartoon by Cruikshank entitled 'Manchester Heroes', made soon after the events at Peterloo. The label 'Peterloo' is a sarcastic reference to the famous Battle of Waterloo where British troops defeated Napoleon. Many were shocked that British troops were used to kill fellow countrymen.*

Source F ▶ *A summary of the Six Acts, the new laws of 1819.*

The Six Acts, 1819

- Possession of weapons banned
- Trials were hurried up. Magistrates could now try cases previously tried by judge and jury
- Magistrates given powers to search homes for weapons or leaflets attacking the government
- New tax put on newspapers to make them more expensive
- Public meetings of over 50 banned
- Marching and weapon practice banned

The Captain Swing Riots

In 1830, 'machine-smashing' started again. This time, however, workers in the countryside attacked farm machinery because farmers began to use machines to do the work that men used to do. This was putting people out of work. Families were starving.

Attacks on farm machinery rapidly spread over the Midlands, East Anglia and Southern England. Farm workers destroyed any machinery they could find, burned down hayricks and sent threatening letters to farmers. These letters were usually signed by 'Captain Swing' (but it is unlikely he existed any more than Ned Ludd did!).

The government took tough action. At a time when there had been a series of bloody revolutions in other European countries, the government wanted to stamp out any violent protest in Britain. The authorities offered £500 for information leading to any arrests and after 2000 people were detained, the

courts dealt severely with them. Sentences included:

- 19 people hanged, mostly for arson
- 644 jailed
- 481 transported to Australia for life
- 7 fined
- 1 whipped

Source G ▼ *A painting of a mob burning hayricks in Kent in 1830.*

The Tolpuddle Martyrs

During the late 1700s, workers in factories and mines faced appalling conditions and low wages. Some workers combined together and formed **trade unions** to fight for better wages and conditions. They refused to work and went on strike if things didn't improve. As you can imagine, most employers didn't like trade unions. They thought the unions encouraged workers to cause trouble … and they thought that if they were forced to pay better wages, it would mean less profit for themselves.

After 1800, trade unions were banned. Politicians – many of whom owned factories, mines and farms – claimed they were dangerous and union meetings could be used to plot rebellions! Unions remained banned until 1824, when the government felt that any threat of rebellion had passed.

In 1833, a group of farm workers met late one night in the village of Tolpuddle in Dorset. They were desperately poor, earning only 35p a week, 15p less than elsewhere. When the local landowners announced plans to bring down wages further, the workers formed their own trade union. At the first meeting, they swore an oath on the Bible and promised to keep their meetings secret. They didn't want the local landowners to find out and sack any workers who belonged to the new union!

Despite the oath of secrecy, the local landowners heard about the new union. Although trade unions were not illegal, there was an old law that banned secret oaths on the Bible! At 6:00am on 24 February 1834, six union members were arrested, marched five miles to Dorchester Prison and charged with 'swearing a secret oath'. In court, the defendants claimed they only wanted to stop their families from starving but the judge decided to 'set an example to the working class'. All six men were sentenced to seven years' transportation to Australia!

But the Tolpuddle men didn't serve their full sentences. There was such a public outcry against the sentences – huge meetings, petitions and a newspaper campaign – that Parliament decided they had been unfairly convicted and returned the men to Britain in 1836.

However, memories of the whole incident stayed in people's memories. Many workers were afraid to join unions for many years afterwards and looked for other ways to improve their lives … soon the Chartist movement would be born!

Source H ▼ *Four of the Tolpuddle Martyrs. After the men had been transported to Australia, their wives received no poor relief (charity donations from local taxes). They were told that, if their husbands could afford to pay the ½p a week to join a union, they could afford to look after their families!*

Source I ▼ *The words of Robert Scott, the man in charge of one of the transported men when he was in Australia.*

> "I understand it was your aim to murder, burn and destroy everything before you. You have been sent over here to be severely punished and no mercy will be shown to you!"

Source J ▼ *A protest meeting against the severe sentences given to the Tolpuddle men. This meeting attracted 30 000 protesters.*

The Chartists

One of the hottest issues in Britain in the 1800s was the right to vote. Mostly it was rich people who were able to vote and ordinary working-class people felt this was unfair. Already unhappy with their lives, millions of ordinary workers felt that if they had the right to vote, perhaps they would be able to 'vote in' politicians who could improve their living and working conditions.

In 1838, a meeting was held in Birmingham to draw up a list of changes to the voting system. Ordinary working people attended the meeting – printers, shopkeepers, tailors, carpenters, shoemakers, newsagents and factory staff. They agreed on six demands. They called this The People's Charter and its supporters became known as the **Chartists** (see **Source K**).

Source K ▼ *What the Chartists wanted. In brackets, it tells you when it was actually achieved.*

The Chartists now set about persuading Parliament to change the voting system. They drew up a huge petition and got thousands of people to sign it to show their support for the changes. When they did this, in 1839 and 1842, twice Parliament turned them down. Each time there were more riots. In Newport, 20 Chartists were killed when soldiers opened fire on 3000 armed coalminers and ironworkers who had met to show their support. 500 Chartists were arrested and imprisoned for over a year and the leaders of the Newport Riots were sentenced to death, although their sentence was reduced to transportation to Australia. Each time the government took tough action, Chartism died down for a few years.

In 1848, there was one final petition containing five million signatures. A huge march across London was planned to deliver the petition to Parliament, but the government acted quickly to prevent riots. 150 000 new policemen were signed up and 100 000 soldiers brought in to protect the city. Even Queen Victoria left London for the safety of the Isle of Wight.

When Parliament received the petition, MPs laughed at it. There were actually fewer than two million signatures and many of them were foreigners.

> ### WISE UP WORDS
> • Luddites   trade union   Chartists

Queen Victoria herself was supposed to have signed it ten times as well as 'April First', 'Cheeky the Marine', 'No cheese', 'Pug nose' and 'Mr Punch'. Fewer Chartists had turned up at the meeting than expected – it had been a very rainy day!

So the Chartists failed. Although nearly all of their demands were adopted over the next seventy years, it seemed that a rainy day had stopped a revolution! But there were other reasons why the movement failed. Life began to improve for many workers and the violence associated with Chartism wasn't popular.

Source L ▶ *A very early photograph of the final huge Chartist meeting, held on Kennington Common, April 1848.*

WORK

1 **a** In your own words, summarise why the government was so worried about the number of protests after 1700.

 b What was the Riot Act of 1715?

2 **a** What did Luddites and Swing Rioters have in common?

 b In what ways were they different?

 c Why do you think they both failed?

 d Why were Ned Ludd and Captain Swing never caught?

3 **a** What did the St Peter's Field demonstrators want?

 b What sort of people went to the demonstration that day?

 c Why do you think the government reacted so violently to the demonstrations?

 d Look at **Source E**. Do you think the artist supported the government's actions that day or not? Give reasons for your answer.

4 **a** Why were the Six Acts passed by Parliament?

 b Why do you think a tax was put on newspapers?

5 **a** Explain what is meant by the word 'martyr'.

 b Do you think 'The Tolpuddle Martyrs' is a suitable label?

 c The following quotes are from newspapers that reported the Tolpuddle case. Would you say the quotes are biased in favour of the men or against them? Give reasons for your answers.

i) 'Trade Unions are, we have no doubt, the most dangerous institutions that were ever permitted to take root in any country.' (*The Morning Post*)

ii) 'Trade Associations should not be attacked by a verdict that shows the treachery of the law by throwing the noose of an Act of Parliament over the heads of sleeping men.' (*The Morning Herald*)

iii) 'A man is never punished in England for that which he is found guilty.' (*The Morning Chronicle*)

iv) 'The case represented an unreasonable and unacceptable stretching of an Act of Parliament. Our judges and lawmakers may rely upon it. This case will never be forgotten.' (*The True Sun*)

6 **a** What did the Chartists want?

 b In your opinion, were the Chartists a success or not? TOP TIP: Try to think short term AND long term!

7 Now copy and complete this table:

	When?	Who were they?	Why did they protest?	How did the government react?	Why did the government react this way?	How were they punished?
Luddites						
Peterloo demonstrators						
Swing Riots						
Tolpuddle Martyrs						
Chartists						

Why did punishments for protesters change after 1850?

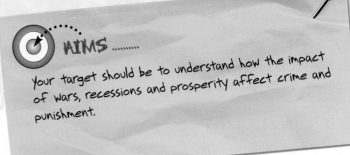

🎯 AIMS ....

Your target should be to understand how the impact of wars, recessions and prosperity affect crime and punishment.

The second half of the nineteenth century saw fewer protests than the first half. There were several reasons for this. For a start, working conditions in factories and mines were improving and there were government programmes to tackle poor living conditions. It was also a time of higher employment and greater prosperity than many people could remember. However, some of the old causes of protest still remained. Pay for working men and women still wasn't particularly good and workers had little power to improve this. And still the majority of men couldn't vote (and no women at all!) so many were angry that they had no say in electing the people who ran their lives.

Read the following four case studies carefully. They each outline a different protest between 1850 and 1930. All the protesters were treated more leniently than you might have come to expect.

A strike in a match factory

London's 'match girls' were amongst the poorest paid workers in the country in the 1880s. Match girls – as the name suggests – produced **phosphorus** matches and one of the largest producers of matches was the Bryant and May factory in the East End of London. Phosphorus is an explosive element that looks like a yellow wax. It is melted, stirred with glue to make a paste and then put on the ends of splints of wood to make matches. Making matches isn't difficult work … but it is highly dangerous. The fumes are lethal and soon attack the teeth of anyone working too closely. Teeth can drop out within months. The disease could spread to the jawbone too and start to rot it away. Sometimes an infected person's jaw had to be completely removed.

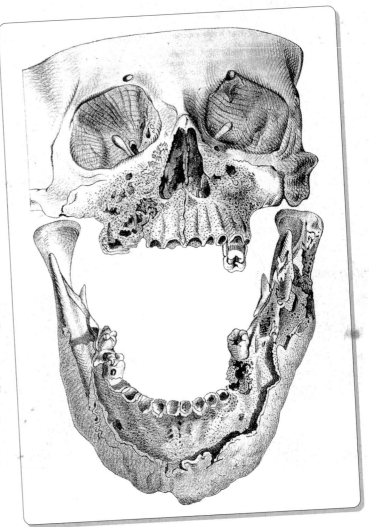

Source A ▶ An illustration of a diseased jawbone from a match girl.

After 1400, many match girls worked in the Bryant and May factory; many had skin diseases from the phosphorus because the factory wasn't equipped with sinks so they couldn't wash their hands. Some workers lost all their hair whilst others shone in the dark because phosphorus was luminous! And they only earned a measly weekly wage of 20p (for a girl) or 40p (for a woman), much of which went on petty fines!

But in June 1888, the match girls went on strike. They had decided that enough was enough. Immediately, these poor uneducated women caused a new sensation and offers of support and money came flooding in. Within two weeks, the girls had been promised better conditions, an end to the fine system and a pay rise!

Other victories by unskilled workers soon followed. In 1889, the threat of a strike by gas workers at the London Gas Company led to their working hours being cut from 70 to 50 a week. Later that year, the London dockworkers, who earned even less than the female match girls, went on strike. They demanded a minimum wage of 2½p an hour. After a long and bitter strike, they got their pay rise too!

Source B ◀ *Match girls on strike.*

Source C ▼ *The Dockers' strike of 1889. Adapted from a modern textbook.*

"The strike lasted five weeks. Hardly anyone expected it to succeed [but] after five weeks, the employers gave in … One vital part of planning the strike was starting on good terms with the police. The Dockers' leaders made every effort to welcome police, talk to them and win their trust. Strikers were careful not to threaten or intimidate other workers as this was against the law … the strikers' peaceful methods won them wide support."

The suffragettes

One of the most famous protest movements of the early twentieth century was the campaign for women's suffrage (suffrage means the right to vote). Since the 1860s, a variety of groups had tried to put pressure on the government to give women the vote. They wrote letters to politicians and organised peaceful meetings … but got nowhere!

In 1903, a small group of women led by Emmeline Pankhurst lost patience with the peaceful methods and formed the Women's Social and Political Union (WSPU). *The Daily Mail* called them the 'suffragettes' and their motto was 'Deeds not words'. Immediately, they began to get public attention by doing illegal acts. They smashed shop windows, set off fire alarms, threw eggs at politicians and chained themselves to railings, including those outside Buckingham Palace (see **Source D**).

Many protesters were arrested … but they were pleased. Photographs of these middle-class women in prison uniform got them much-needed publicity! Their time in prison gave them another weapon too – the hunger strike. To begin with, the government released women who wouldn't eat but later they were force-fed by stuffing a tube up their nose or down their throat to make them eat.

Source D ▶ *The suffragettes did all they could to get public attention, including chaining themselves to railings.*

Source E ▶ *Many women were arrested for their behaviour. Many reacted by going on hunger strikes but the government fought back by force-feeding them. They would pour soup through a tube up their nose or down their throat!*

By 1910, some politicians began working for a change in the law to allow women to vote – but still too many MPs were against it. The suffragettes responded by getting more violent. They let off bombs, burned down churches, cut telephone wires and poured acid onto golf courses. During a visit to Dublin, an axe was thrown at the Prime Minister, narrowly missing him. Most famous of all, Emily Davison was killed when she ran onto the racetrack during the 1913 Derby in an attempt to stop the King's horse!

By 1914, more and more people were getting worried about the increasing violence. The government hit back with prison sentences for window-breakers or any protesters refusing to pay their fines. If women went on hunger strike, their 'cat and mouse law' allowed their release so they could get better ... but they would be arrested as soon as they were healthy again.

In August 1914, when war broke out in Europe, Mrs Pankhurst told her suffragettes to stop all action and called them in to help win the war. As a result of the effort made by women during World War One, all women over the age of 30 were given the vote.

Conchies

During World War One, the government introduced a law that said that all men between the ages of 18 and 41 could be forced to join the army. This was known as conscription. Two and a half million men joined up as a result of this ... but over 15 000

refused to join because they said they were **conscientious objectors** (COs). This meant they refused to fight for religious or moral reasons – they felt it just wasn't right to be involved in a conflict where human beings killed each other. Many COs, or Conchies as they were nicknamed, agreed to do other work, such as working in hospitals behind the front lines or driving injured soldiers around. But over 1000 refused to take any part in the war at all. All of them went on trial and if they still refused to fight, they went to prison. Seventy-one of them died behind bars as a result of poor treatment. They also had their right to vote taken away!

Source F ▾ *A copy of a postcard published in 1917 showing the life of a CO in prison.*

During World War Two, the government was less harsh on COs. Prison was only used as a last resort. Instead, they were put to work on farms or in factories – still work related to winning the war but jobs that avoided direct conflict. Yet public attitudes to the Conchies were always less than sympathetic! Many were spat at in the street, sacked from their jobs and even beaten up.

Source G ⬆ *A volunteer driver during the General Strike 'protected' by a police escort.*

The General Strike, 1926

In 1925, mine-owners proposed a cut in wages for their workers and an increase in their hours. The miners' leader famously replied 'Not a penny off the pay, not a minute on the day!' as he turned down their proposal. When mine-owners pushed forward with their plans, the workers in other industries – transport, steel, iron, chemicals, gas and printing – said they'd strike in support of their fellow workers. In other words, there would be a **general strike**. The strike began on Monday 3 May. On 4 May, there were hardly any trains or trams running. Power stations stopped working and there were no newspapers. As time went on though, volunteer workers began to do the work that regular workers were refusing to do (see **Source G**). There was some violence as a result – buses were set on fire and there were clashes between police and strikers – but on the whole, the General Strike was relatively peaceful.

On 12 May 1926, however, union leaders suddenly called off the strike. Their 'strike fund' was running low and some feared a possible revolution. Strike leaders never wanted a revolution! The miners decided to fight on alone but eventually returned to work – for less money and longer hours. From 1927, General Strikes were made illegal – this is a law that is still in force!

FACT *Arrests*

Nearly 5000 arrests were made during the General Strike, mainly for public disorder offences. Over 1000 people were sent to prison for between four and eight years when they derailed a train in Northumberland.

WORK

1 Suggest reasons why the second half of the nineteenth century saw fewer protests than the first.

2 Look at **Source A**. Why is this jawbone disfigured?

3 Look at **Source D**. What is this woman doing ... and why is she doing it?

4 **a** Look at **Source F**. Why is the man in the postcard being treated in this way?

   b Do you think the artist who drew the postcard was for or against conscientious objectors? Give reasons for your answer.

5 Look at **Source G**. Why is the policeman travelling on the London bus in this way?

6 **a** Copy and complete the table below.

PROTESTERS	DATE	REASON FOR PROTEST	HOW DID THE GOVERNMENT REACT?	SUCCESS OR NOT?	GIVE REASONS FOR YOUR ANSWERS
Match girls					
Suffragettes					
Conchies					
General Strikers					

   b Why do you think protesters were punished more harshly in the early 1800s than they were after 1850?

7 **a** List a few causes of popular protests today.

   b Who deals with protests today?

   c In what ways are protesters punished today?

SUMMARY

- Protests occurred for lots of reasons: high food prices, issues surrounding the right to vote and unemployment were three of the main causes. Whenever the economic conditions in the country improved, the number of riots and protests declined.

- The methods of protest were wide-ranging – destruction of property, rioting, mass meetings, petitions and marches. The government used the police and the army to deal with them. They also introduced new laws such as the Riot Act.

- Up until the mid-nineteenth century, protesters were punished severely – hanging, imprisonment or transportation for example. As the century wore on, Parliament didn't feel as threatened just because workers were protesting about bad pay or conditions, so punishments were less severe. There were also lots of groups protesting about different issues – the government couldn't force all of these groups to stop.

Into the twenty-first century

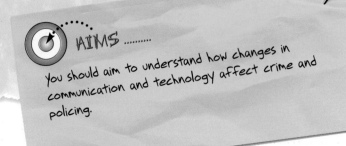

AIMS ....

You should aim to understand how changes in communication and technology affect crime and policing.

STOP PRESS! HOLD THE FRONT PAGE!

CRIME RATE KEEPS ON RISING

During the twentieth century, and into the twenty-first, the crime rate has risen and risen. As Britain became a more media-centred society, newspapers and television programmes focused on this 'crime wave' as it gradually became more of a hot political issue.

Crime and punishment remains a hot political issue today – some call for better policing and tougher prisons, whilst others blame the government for the problems and focus on a general decline in moral values.

So why has the crime rate increased? Is it fair to call it a 'crime wave'? And how has the government responded to the crime rate in terms of policing and prisons?

The crime rate

Look carefully at **Source A**. It shows all the crimes known to police per 100 000 of the population between 1870 and 1990. The graph has even been adjusted to take the rising population into account! It doesn't take a genius to work out the crime rate has increased dramatically, especially since about 1950.

Source A ▶

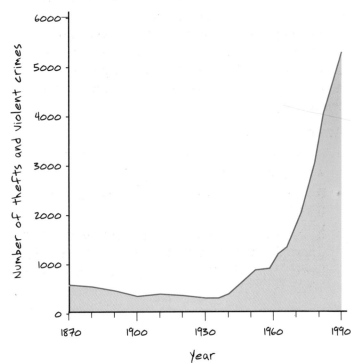

Now look at **Source B**. This shows the numbers of murders, burglaries and thefts known to the police between 1900 and 2000.

Source B ▾

Date	Murder/Manslaughter	Burglary	Theft
1900	312	3812	63 604
1910	291	6499	76 044
1920	313	6863	77 417
1930	300	11 169	110 159
1950	315	29 834	334 222
1960	282	46 591	537 003
1970	393	190 597	952 666
1980	620	294 375	1 463 469
1996	681	1 101 000	2 280 000

But do these figures tell the whole story? **Sources A** and **B** are based on recorded crime, that is, crimes that people have gone into a police station and reported. But these sorts of statistics are problematic! Not all people report crimes for example, so the real figures could be even higher. A survey in the early 1980s even suggested that there were 12, yes 12, times more cases of vandalism than was actually reported!

British Crime Survey

For a number of reasons, people don't always report crimes so they don't get recorded in crime figures. The British Crime Survey (BCS) was set up to ask people about their actual experiences of crime rather than what they had reported to the police. Many believe that BCS figures give a very accurate picture of crime levels and trends across the country.

According to the BCS:

- In the year 2004/05, the total number of crimes was around 11 million.
- Total crime peaked in 1995 and has since fallen by 44%.
- In 2004/05, nearly 25% of the population were the victim of some type of crime. This has fallen from a high of nearly 40% of the population in 1995.

Source C ▾ *'Total crime' figures from the British Crime Survey. The survey shows us many interesting details. For example, whilst elderly people felt they were the most at risk from violent crime, it is in fact the under 30s that are thirteen times more likely to be the victim of a violent crime than an older person.*

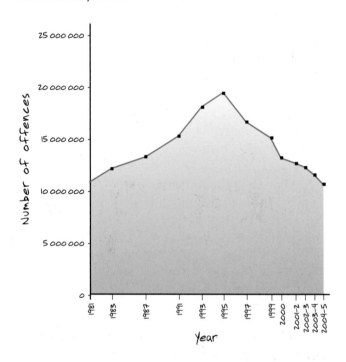

New crimes

Some analysts put the increase in crime in the twentieth century down to factors such as new technology. Invent computers, for example, and you have computer crimes such as 'hacking'. Invent credit cards and you have card fraud and identity theft. Mobile phones have caused a huge increase in attacks on 11–16 year olds between the hours of three and five o'clock as they walk home from school with their mobile phone pressed to their ear, oblivious to the fact that someone wants to steal it!

However, the most startling impact that new technology has had on crime statistics must be the invention of the motor car. Suddenly, you have lots of new crime associated with it – car theft, speeding, drink driving, joy riding, driving without insurance and tax and so on. In fact, in 2005, there were 4 350 000 car crimes, including the theft of over 214 000 cars. Car theft is now one of the country's biggest crime categories – and one of the police's biggest headaches.

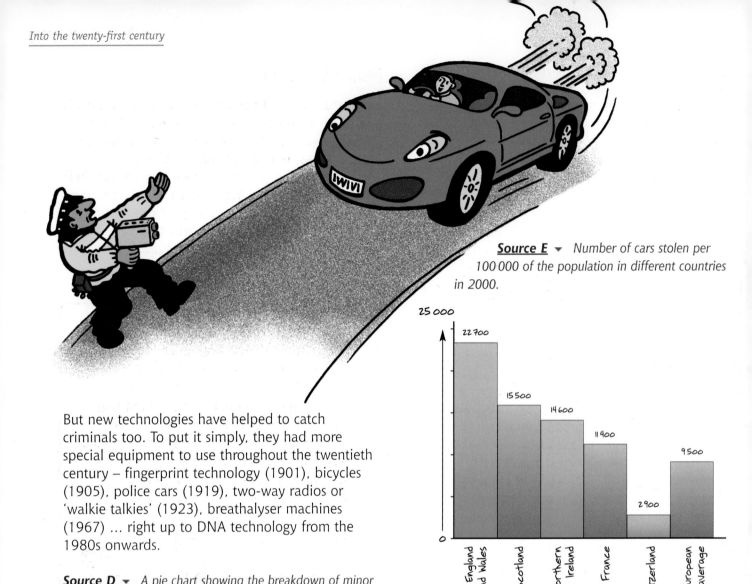

Source E ▾ *Number of cars stolen per 100 000 of the population in different countries in 2000.*

But new technologies have helped to catch criminals too. To put it simply, they had more special equipment to use throughout the twentieth century – fingerprint technology (1901), bicycles (1905), police cars (1919), two-way radios or 'walkie talkies' (1923), breathalyser machines (1967) … right up to DNA technology from the 1980s onwards.

Source D ▾ *A pie chart showing the breakdown of minor incidents dealt with by the police in Birmingham in 1996.*

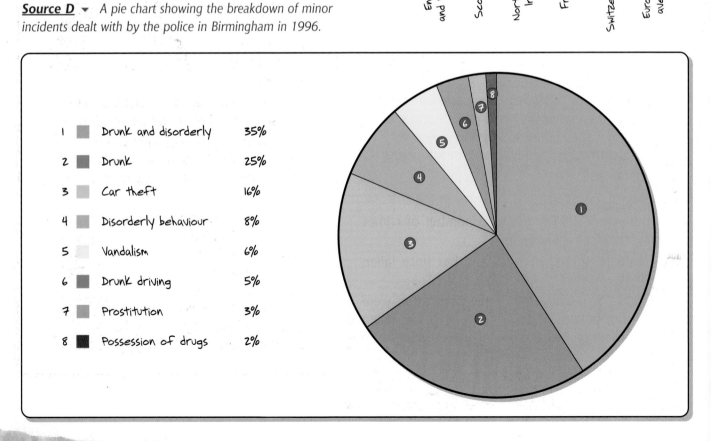

1	▇	Drunk and disorderly	35%
2	▇	Drunk	25%
3	▇	Car theft	16%
4	▇	Disorderly behaviour	8%
5	▇	Vandalism	6%
6	▇	Drunk driving	5%
7	▇	Prostitution	3%
8	▇	Possession of drugs	2%

Source F ▾ *A newspaper headline from
the* Sunday Times *on 18 June 2006. Today, crime sells
newspapers and wins television audiences (count how many
programmes feature the police, murder investigations or the
courts). As a result, many believe we are living in the middle
of a crime wave. A 1997 survey of 11 countries showed one
in three Brits felt unsafe out alone at night compared to one
in four Americans, one in four Frenchmen and one in ten
Swedes!*

Crisis as prisons run out of cells

Steven Swinford

THE chief inspector of prisons has warned that Britain's overcrowded jails are close to putting up "house full" notices and having to turn away newly convicted criminals.

Anne Owers said that with fewer than 1,800 places left from a total of 79,500, prisons could soon "hit the buffers" and be unable to take any more offenders.

With thousands held in overcrowded conditions, including three to a cell, a further 1,800 would put the system in breach of health and safety laws. If present trends continue, it would reach breaking point by mid-September.

"We are looking at a system where prison numbers are rising inside what is already a hugely pressured area," Owers said in an interview with The Sunday Times. "That may hit the buffers soon at a point where there are not any more spaces. I think the point will come at which prisons have to put up 'house full' notices."

The warning comes at a bad time for Tony Blair, who last week signalled that the government was planning to increase the time serious offen

West Midlands because two jails have been converted to take men. All but 19 of the 139 prisons in England and Wales are within 50 spaces of being full.

The jail population reached 77,785 on Friday, with just 1,715 spaces left. Since the beginning of May the overall prison population has increased by an average of 148 inmates a week.

The Home Office has refused to detail any contingency plans. However, it is understood they may include the early release of criminals guilty of less serious offences and holding of prisoners in police cells at a cost of £363 a night per inmate.

According to Owers, the rising population means there are fewer resources for rehabilitating offenders.

"I want prisons to be effective," she said. "I don't want prisons where there aren't the resources to deal with the underlying causes of offending."

Last week Lord Falconer, the lord chancellor, tried to defuse the row over "soft sentences" by calling for a review of the one-third discount offenders earn for pleading guilty. His comments came after John Reid, the home secretary, criticised the sentence of Craig Sweeney, a serial pae-

Punishing crime

Up to the nineteenth century, criminals were usually treated as worthless, sinful people who got what they deserved in rotten prisons. As the century wore on, there was more of a belief in reforming criminals and the prisons in which they served their sentences. In the twentieth century, a whole host of reforms greatly changed the way prisoners were punished. Look carefully at **Source G**. It shows the gradual change in prisoner punishment.

Source G ▾ *Some key dates in the history of punishment.*

1907: Probation introduced – an alternative to prison. Criminals reported once a week to the police station. If they didn't re-offend, there was no further punishment.

1914: Longer to pay fines – this meant that people who had been fined could take longer to pay rather than be sent to prison.

1937: First 'open prison' – trusted adult prisoners were sent to these 'prisons without bars' to serve out their sentences.

1962: Birching (whipping) was stopped.

1965: Capital punishment (hanging for murder) was abolished.

1967: Parole introduced – prisoners were released early if they had behaved in jail.

1972: Community service introduced – criminals could be sentenced to help out on community projects instead of spending time in jail.

1999 onwards: Electronic tagging – a type of probation. Criminals, upon release from prison, wear an electronic bracelet that allows the police to know where they are at any time.

Source H ▲ *During the 1980s and 1990s, some of Britain's prisons were filled to bursting point. Prison staff shortages meant that in some places, prisoners were spending 23 hours a day in their cells with no education programmes and little exercise. There were riots in some prisons, notably in Strangeways Prison in Manchester in 1990. One solution to overcrowding was the use of prison ships, last used in the 1800s. This one, pictured in 1997, was moored off the Dorset coast and held 500 prisoners.*

Source I ▶ *Britain's rising prison population. In the 1980s, Britain had the fourth highest proportion of prisoners in Europe, with the prison population growing at a rate of 350 prisoners a week. More prisons have been built since 1990 and even 'private prisons' have opened, run by companies on behalf of the government.*

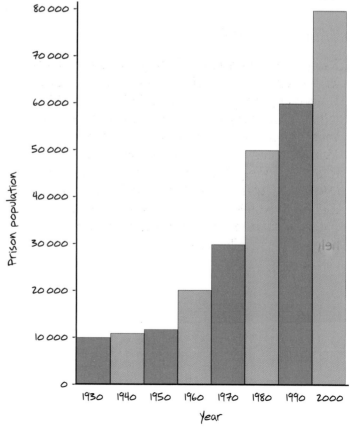

Young criminals

Many special measures affecting younger criminals have been introduced since 1900. The first borstal – a juvenile prison – was opened in Kent in 1902, followed by many others. These were replaced by Youth Detention Centres for under 21s in 1983. In 1933, the age of criminal responsibility was raised to the age of eight, and then raised further to ten (1963) and then 14 in 1969. Also in that year, specialist juvenile courts, supervision and care orders were introduced as a way of reforming and helping young offenders.

WORK

1 **a** In general terms, what has happened to the crime rate in the twentieth century?

   b Can you suggest reasons for this?

2 **a** What do you think is meant by the term 'new crime'?

   b Make a list of new crimes and old crimes.

   c Car crime would be regarded as a 'new crime'. For the next few weeks, keep a list of crimes reported in your national or local newspaper. No excuses here, we all get a local newspaper delivered through our door or have access to a library! For each crime, decide whether it is a new crime or an old crime.

3 **a** In what ways has the invention of the motor car, for example, contributed to the increased crime rate?

   b Look at **Source D**. What percentage of the minor incidents in Birmingham in 1996 involved the motor car in some way?

4 Work with a partner. You have each been asked to write a crime feature for the national newspaper you work for.

   • One of you works for a 'tabloid' newspaper and you must write a sensational story that will sell as many papers as possible.

   • The other works for a different newspaper whose editor wants a balanced report.

   Both of you are limited to 350 words. You can include two pictures or graphs at most and must have an eye-catching headline. They must both be based on the same story.

5 Look carefully at these two statements:

   i) 'The treatment of prisoners has changed for the better in the twentieth century. It is far better to reform them so they can return to society as better people.'

   ii) 'Prisoners get it easy today. The prison system has gone soft on them.'

   Which statement do you agree with more? Try to make points in your argument and use examples from the text wherever possible. You have been asked here to express an opinion – to do it properly, you need to back up your arguments!

New crimes

AIMS

Over the next four pages, aim to:
- identify key crimes in the twenty-first century;
- form opinions on whether certain crimes are new or just old crimes with a new identity.

There are many, many different types of crime. But the most common type of crime across all periods has always been theft. Crimes like murder and violent or sexual assault have always been the ones that have grabbed all the headlines but they have only ever made up a small percentage of the overall crime figures.

However, every period studied – from Roman Times to the present day – tends to have what you might call 'new crimes'. For example, when Strict Puritans ran the country in the 1650s, playing football on a Sunday became a 'new crime'. In the 1700s, highway robbery was the 'new crime' punishable by death. And the use of motor cars in the twentieth century made drink driving and speeding another couple of these so-called 'new crimes'.

But are some of these 'new crimes' not actually new at all? Is highway robbery just theft for example – one of the oldest and most common crimes of all? Even taking it right up to date with the very modern crimes of computer hacking and mobile phone cloning – aren't these two very modern crimes also just theft?

Take a look through the following information on some of today's so-called 'new crimes'. Are they really new crimes at all? Or are they just new opportunities for old crimes?

Computer crime

'Cyber crime' is one of the twenty-first century's fastest-growing crimes. As so much information is kept on computers, criminals have been able to use them to steal money from bank accounts and carry out identity theft by 'hacking' into private records of businesses and individuals to steal information (see **Source A**).

Source A ▶ *From an online article on the BBC website (December, 2003). In June 2004, government ministers proposed an increase in the length of jail sentences for 'computer hackers'.*

"This year [2003] has seen a rise in malicious programmes written to steal information that criminals could use to plunder net bank accounts or to carry out identity theft.

Viruses used to be essentially pointless, like electronic graffiti … but now we are seeing worms that try to extract financial information from users. For instance, Mimail-J [a computer virus] poses as a message from Internet payment firm PayPal and asks for credit card information and Bugbear-B [another virus] attempts to steal keystrokes relating to credit cards in use online … there are now 86 000 known viruses and about 700 new ones being created every week."

Tobacco smuggling

Smoking is the single greatest cause of premature death and preventable illness in Britain … so reducing it has been one of the government's key health objectives for many years. Increasing the price of cigarettes through taxation has been one way the government has tried to reduce the number of smokers, but the price increases have meant cigarettes bought in from abroad have been a lot cheaper in comparison … so they have been smuggled in, in huge numbers to sell illegally!

In 2005, it was estimated that one in five cigarettes smoked in Britain had been smuggled in. Some estimates put the figure at one in three. A government minister claimed that this costs the country £2½ billion in lost tax revenue a year … and puts vast sums of money into the hands of criminal smuggling gangs (see **Source B**).

Source B ▾ *The proposed government strategy for reducing tobacco smuggling.*

Government strategy for cutting down tobacco smuggling

- More hi-tech scanners in ports.
- Clearly marked UK cigarette packets, making smuggled cigarettes easier to spot.
- Increased punishments for those caught with smuggled goods.
- More customs officers at sea ports, airports and so on.
- Huge publicity campaign outlining the fact that the profit from tobacco smuggling is used by the gangs to commit other crimes – drug smuggling for example.

Terrorism

There has been the threat of terrorist violence in Britain for many years. However, since the attacks by al-Qaeda (an Islamic fundamentalist terror group) on the World Trade Center in America in September 2001, the threat has increased massively. In recent years, a series of explosions ripped through London's transport system (see **Source C**) and a terror plot to hi-jack passenger jets over London was discovered and stopped in 2006.

Britain itself has been on a 'severe' or 'critical' terrorist threat since 2001 and the added security and ever-present menace of bombings has made terrorism a constant worry and huge drain on police and security-service resources.

Source C ▾ *The bombed-out remains of a London bus after the terrorist attacks on London on 7 July 2005. Three young men, members of al-Qaeda, blew themselves up on London tube trains, whilst a fourth exploded his bomb on this bus in Woburn Place. In total, over 52 people were killed and 700 injured.*

Source D ▾ *Threat levels are descriptions that give an indication of the likelihood of a terrorist attack. The five threat levels are based on current intelligence, recent events and what is known about terrorist intentions and abilities. You can view Britain's current terror threat level on www.mi5.gov.uk.*

Threat levels issued by MI5

LOW – an attack is unlikely.

MODERATE – an attack is possible but not likely

SUBSTANTIAL – an attack is a strong possibility

SEVERE – an attack is highly likely

CRITICAL – an attack is expected immediately

Source E ▾ *A member of an Army bomb disposal unit attends the scene as a house is searched in connection with investigations into the London bombings in Birmingham.*

Source F ▾ *From the MI5 website.*

"The UK is a prominent target for international terrorist groups. There have been bomb and gun attacks on British citizens and interests in a number of countries over the last few years, as well as targets in the UK itself:

- November 2003 – al-Qaeda attacked the British Consulate and HSBC building in Istanbul, killing 27 people including three British citizens;

- September 2004 – A British national residing in Saudi Arabia was killed in a Riyadh shopping centre by al-Qaeda gunmen;

- October 2004 – British engineer Kenneth Bigley was murdered in Iraq by the al-Qaeda in Iraq group;

- March 2005 – A British teacher was killed in a car bomb explosion in Doha, Qatar;

- July 2005 – Four suicide bombers attacked the London transport system, killing themselves and 52 other passengers. A subsequent attempted attack failed, with no casualties being caused."

People smuggling and human trafficking

People smuggling is a term that describes the transportation of people across international borders to a non-official entry point of a destination country for financial gain. In recent years, criminal gangs have targeted this 'trade' and made vast sums of money from people who pay them in order to be smuggled into Britain.

Source G ▾ *An image released by the Metropolitan Police in London shows the capability of the truck X-ray machine similar to those based at the English and French ports of Dover and Calais. On Tuesday 11 October 2005, a series of raids took place across London at dawn to smash a multi-million pound people smuggling empire regarded as one of the biggest in Europe.*

Source H ▾ *A description of people smuggling by Interpol, the international police network.*

"People smuggling has become the preferred trade of a growing number of criminal networks worldwide that are showing an increasing sophistication in regard to moving larger numbers of people at higher profits than ever."

Human trafficking is different from people smuggling. When people are smuggled, they usually pay a fee and are then free to go when they reach their destination. Trafficking invokes the use of physical force, fraud and deception to obtain and transport people. Women in particular are 'trafficked'. They are promised good jobs and education but are usually forced to work as prostitutes. Again, the traffickers make huge amounts of money.

Source I ▾ *From a newspaper article.*

August 2006

BIRMINGHAM POST

POLICE RESCUE CITY SEX SLAVES

Several women, brought to Birmingham and forced to work as prostitutes, have been rescued by police … 19 women in total, from ten countries including Albania, Kosovo and Latvia, were found to be working as prostitutes in Cuddles massage parlour in the Bearwood area of the city … several people suspected of human trafficking will go on trial next year.

WORK

1 Write a one-line definition of each of the following:
   i) cyber crime
   ii) tobacco smuggling
   iii) terrorism
   iv) people smuggling
   v) human trafficking

2 Which of the crimes on these pages would you regard as:
   i) new crimes?
   ii) new ways of committing old crimes?
   Make sure you give reasons for your answers, using examples from your studies.

3 **a** Monitor the newspapers and TV news programmes for a set amount of time (a week, for example). Make a list of the different types of crime.

   b For each of the crimes, describe whether you think it is a new crime, or just an old, common crime with a new method of committing it.

'Call the police!'

AIMS

Aim to:
- identify the image of the police;
- understand how the role of the police force has changed during the twentieth century.

Ask most people what the role of a police officer is and you would probably get replies like 'to catch criminals', 'to prevent crime' and 'to arrest people'. All of these responses are true ... but the role of a modern police officer is much more complex than that.

So what is the role of today's police officer? How has that role changed? And how has their image changed over the years?

Today's police officers work with the public, businesses and organisations to reduce crime and the fear of crime. It is a citizen-focused job that responds to the needs of individuals and communities. Their role is incredibly diverse (see **Source A**). In fact, a survey in the 1990s revealed that only 20% of calls made to the police were crime-related. The rest concerned things like loud music, reporting accidents, consumer advice and lost property!

The work of a police officer is so varied that they cannot be skilled at every one of their roles. Preventing terrorism, for example, is a specialist role and an Anti-Terrorist Squad was set up in 1971. A Fraud Squad, dealing with criminal deception, 'con-men' and so on was set up in 1946. There are other specialist roles in areas such as firearms support, child protection and criminal investigation (CID).

Source A ▶ *The National Police Training College was set up in 1947 and there are at least 14 weeks of basic training. Initial training activities include the following and these reflect some of the more common jobs a police officer is likely to do.*

Jobs of a police officer

- conduct patrol duties on foot, by car and bicycle;
- respond to calls from the public to assist at incidents (such as criminal activity, domestic disputes, fires and public disorder);
- attend road-related incidents including collision scenes, vehicle checkpoints and traffic offences;
- deliver death and hospital messages to families;
- keep the peace at public meetings, events, processions, trade disputes or strikes;
- gather evidence and take statements;
- interview suspects, victims and witnesses;
- search individuals, personal property, vehicles, premises and land;
- conduct arrests, whilst having regard for human rights, security and the health and safety of individuals detained, members of the public, colleagues and self;
- administer custody procedures as an arresting officer;
- gather, record and analyse intelligence to achieve community safety and crime reduction objectives;
- prepare crime reports;
- attend and give evidence in court;
- develop and maintain community relations.

Source B ▼ *A police officer talks to a couple of 'naughty boys' in North Kensington, London, in the 1960s. During this time, the public image of the police was at its height. They were seen as trustworthy and fair, officers who used their common sense whenever possible yet could be really tough with hardened criminals. Popular TV shows like Dixon of Dock Green (ask your grandparents!) reinforced this popular image.*

Source C ▼ *From an interview with David Ashman from Halesowen, West Midlands, who spoke of his childhood memories of the local 'bobby on the beat'. As the motor car increased in use in the 1970s, the 'bobby on the beat' began to disappear. However, foot patrols were reintroduced by many forces in the 1990s as public demand grew for the reassuring sight of a police officer in their community.*

"When I was a kid in the late 1950s, the local bobby caught me and a mate chalking cartoon pictures of the butcher's wife on a wall near my house. I remember him getting off his pushbike and telling us he knew where we lived and we had half an hour to wash it off. To be honest, we half expected a clip round the ear for our sins. It was common practice for them to do that back then. You wouldn't ever tell your parents because they'd give you another one.

Anyway, we washed it off in record time and lived the next few weeks in fear of the local bobby coming to my house and telling my dad."

Source E ▼ *A photograph of inspector Dennis Bell, who had just been hit by a flying brick during the Brixton riots. By then, the friendly 'father figure' image of the police had mostly disappeared.*

Source D ▶ *A photograph of the Brixton riots, April 1981. The 1980s were a low-point in the image of the police. A report into the riots concluded that an important cause was that the police had 'lost touch' with the communities they served and had lost their respect through alleged racism and aggressive policing.*

The police force 'reborn'

The low point in the image of Britain's police was the 1980s. As crime figures rose, the police were put under more pressure to solve crime. Teams of policemen speeding up to incidents in their cars and vans and arresting lots of people became a more common sight than the 'bobby on the beat' using his common sense to clear up crime. Some officers even faked evidence and forced confessions to get results. Scandals like the cases of the 'Guildford Four' and the 'Birmingham Six' – men falsely convicted of crimes – gradually eroded the public image of the police. Even 'cop shows' like *The Sweeney* (again, ask your parents!) presented the world of police work as a tough and violent one where police officers were prepared to cut corners in order to get results.

Source F ▶

Armed police patrol Whitehall in London as the British government discuss how to strengthen anti-terror laws, July 2005. Specialist rapid response units have been incorporated into the police force in recent years.

Source G ▶ *In areas where there is a neighbourhood watch scheme, there have been significant drops in the crime rate.*

THIS IS A
NEIGHBOURHOOD WATCH
AREA

By the 1990s though, the government began to introduce measures to help rebuild the public image of the police. Community links were improved by offering crime prevention advice in the form of 'neighbourhood watch' schemes or visiting schools and youth clubs to talk about their work.

There was a large recruitment drive to bring in more female officers and men and women from ethnic minorities. Foot and horse patrols were increased when research showed that the general public felt safer when they saw police officers walking around the streets. In 2003, special community officers – dressed very similarly to police officers and with direct radio links to them – were introduced to increase street safety and improve links with local communities.

WORK

1   Look at **Source A.** Using no more than 50 words, write a job description for today's police officers.

2   Look at **Source C.**
   i)   Why was the boy in this source 'in trouble' with the police?
   ii) What punishment did he expect?
   iii) Do you think it is right or wrong that police officers in the 1950s and 1960s should give misbehaving youngsters 'a clip round the ear'? Give reasons for your answer.

3   **a** What image of the police do you get from TV, films, books, magazines and newspapers? Try to give examples if you can.

   b Copy and complete the following chart.

	IMAGE OF THE POLICE
1950s	
1980s	
Today	

   c What is your attitude to the police? Write down at least three statements.

What sort of crime is 'racism'?

Look at **Source A** carefully. The chart shows the number of recorded racial attacks in England and Wales in recent years.

Source A ▼ *These figures certainly suggest a sharp increase in racial attacks. But, like all statistics, be careful not to completely take them at face value. For example, the figures show recorded attacks. In the past, some of these attacks reported to the police would not have been recorded. They may have been dealt with informally or 'off the record'. In more recent years, the police have recorded more crime (computers make it easier) and for certain crimes, like racial attacks, there has been pressure to record them properly. As a result, perhaps be careful not to think that racist attacks have increased enormously since 1988 ... perhaps they happened just as often back then – but now they are recorded better!*

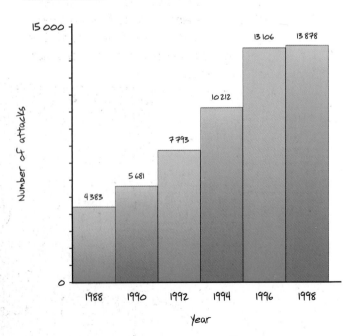

Pause for thought

Why do you think that racially motivated crimes have become more common in recent years?

So what is racial harassment?

According to the Commission for Racial Equality (CRE), 'racial harassment' is 'verbal or physical violence towards individuals or groups on grounds of their colour, race, nationality or ethnic or national origin, where the victims believe the aggression is racially motivated and/or there is evidence of racial motivation.' Attacks on property are also included in this definition.

Most victims of 'race crime' are members of ethnic minority groups, with the most commonly attacked group being the Asian community. 98% of attacks against Pakistanis, 93% of attacks against Indians and 87% of those against Afro-Caribbeans are committed by white offenders. Nearly half of attacks are committed by 16 to 25 year olds.

Yet despite the figures in **Source A**, thousands of racial incidents still go unreported to the police. Figures researched by the CRE in 1996 suggested that only 15% of incidents were reported to the police by the Pakistani community. The same research project showed that 50% of Indians and 34% of black people reported incidents.

"Under the Race Relations Act of 1976, it became an offence to practise racial discrimination in education, employment, housing and the provision of goods and services. Both direct and indirect discrimination are banned. In other words, obvious discrimination is not allowed (very offensive speech or action and 'incitement to racial hatred'). Neither is a more subtle form, in which conditions are laid down which no member of an ethnic minority could ever meet.

Also, it became an offence if the effect of what was done or said was to discriminate against someone, even if that was not the intention.

In 2000, after the Stephen Lawrence Report [see later], this law was tightened by the Labour Government. Now its scope is extended to the police, to those working in the prison service and other groups.

Under the Public Order Act of 1986, the law on racial incitement was tightened, so that it is an offence to act in such a way as to 'stir up' hatred against any racial group in Great Britain."

The murder of Stephen Lawrence

On 22 April 1993, a black British teenager named Stephen Lawrence was waiting at a bus stop in Eltham, south east London, with his friend Duwayne Brookes. Stephen was attacked by a group of young white males and suffered two deep stab wounds that cut major arteries, severed a vein and penetrated a lung. One of the attackers shouted a racial slur as he was attacked. Despite his injuries, Stephen managed to run 130 yards up the road but collapsed and bled to death soon after.

Several youths were investigated by the police but the cases were dropped because of a lack of evidence. By then, the case had attracted national attention and in 1996, Stephen's family took out a private prosecution against five men suspected of his murder. After the case against two was dropped, and the other three were acquitted, the *Daily Mail*

named all five suspects and labelled them as 'murderers', challenging them to sue the newspaper for **libel**. To date, the men have not sued the newspaper (see **Source C**).

In 1999, the report of an inquiry into the case (known as the Stephen Lawrence Report) was heavily critical of the way the police carried out their investigation. The report called the police 'racist' and criticised the errors made in the murder investigation. Over 70 changes to policing and the law were recommended. Indeed, changes to British law actually took place as a direct result of the report – for example, cases are now allowed to be brought back to trial if new evidence is found, even if the defendants have already been found 'not guilty' of the crime. This was banned before the Stephen Lawrence Report!

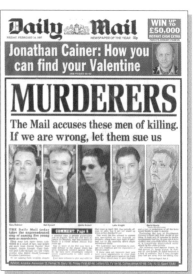

Source E ▶ *A stone plaque marks the spot where Stephen Lawrence died. His mother, Doreen Lawrence, said, 'I would like Stephen to be remembered as a young man who had a*

future. He was well loved and had he been given the chance to survive, maybe he would have been the one to bridge the gap between black and white because he didn't distinguish between black or white. He saw people as people.'

Race relations in Burnley, 2001

In the summer months of 2001, there was rioting in some northern towns like Bradford, Leeds, Oldham and Burnley. They were quickly labelled 'race riots' because the clashes took place between gangs of white and Asian youths. Some of the more serious violence took place in Burnley, a Lancashire mill town with no apparent history of racial tension. Car windows were smashed, pubs vandalised, individuals beaten up and property burned (see **Source F**).

In most of the towns affected by rioting, about 10% of the population are from an ethnic minority (mainly from Bangladesh and Pakistan). Also, white people and Asians tend to live in their own separate 'areas' within each town and are mutually suspicious of each other. In some places, the population is over 90% Asian. In recent years, the British National Party (a party that supports racial discrimination and opposes immigration) has gained lots of support. It won a surprise 11.2% of the local vote in the 2001 general election! Look carefully at **Sources G, H, I** and **J**. Each offers either a viewpoint or report on the rioting.

Source G ▾ *From the Guardian, 26 June 2001.*

"Past the shattered traffic lights, torched cars and the shell of a petrol-bombed pub, a white man in his 20s ran down the road, shouting: 'Racists have put it on the internet — "If you love your country come to Burnley". The bloody bastards.'

An Asian man shrugged. 'Welcome to Sarajevo,' he said.

Police were on the streets of Burnley, in Lancashire, again last night following three consecutive evenings of racial violence, culminating on Sunday night with the petrol bombing of a pub and skirmishes between 200 whites and Asians armed with bricks and hammers. These included some whites allegedly making Nazi salutes and shouting: 'Niggers out'."

Source H ▾ *This is what one Asian man is reported to have said immediately after the riots.*

"This is nothing like Oldham [another town hit by race riots]. Whites and Asians all socialise together. My fiancée is white. No one expects any more fighting. But if pub windows are smashed, there will probably be retaliations on our property. Racial attacks — that's what Britain's all about isn't it?"

Source I ▾ *Adapted from an article by Michael Hindley, a Labour Party MEP from 1984 to 1999.*

"Underachievement and lack of prospects have provoked feelings of resentment and alienation. Poverty, and not race, is the main problem."

Source F ◀ *In 2001, riots in Bradford revealed tensions between white and Asian communities.*

Source J ▾ *The Asian Deputy Mayor of Burnley.*

"It's madness. The only winners are the British National Party. They have got what they wanted. The racial violence we haven't seen in Burnley before has begun and community relations have been dealt a severe blow. It'll take a long time to repair it."

Investigations following the race riots focused on the need to promote good race relations by drawing people together to discuss how to end the segregation of the white and Asian communities. Attention also fell on the poor living conditions and facilities in the areas and on the startling amount of youth crime committed on the streets.

Several things have been done all over the country to try to break the circle of deprivation and violence which many people felt contributed to the feelings of boredom and discontentment felt by many young people:

- 'School beat officers' were appointed to whom children can take their problems.
- A 'Karrot Scheme' was introduced in which good citizenship was rewarded with fun trips.
- Youth clubs have been created.
- Play areas (skate parks and so on) have been built to give youngsters a place to go to encourage them to take pride in their community.

Yet results still claim that crime and racial tension continues on some estates – and in some cases, as much as before. Gangs still hang around dealing drugs, and theft, vandalism and assault are as common as ever.

Also, the BNP still attracts support in local elections and uses its website to present itself as the face of white Britain and to organise meetings and demonstrations. And race crime still happens! It seems as if the 'hot topic' of race relations and how to improve them is set to run and run.

Pause for thought

- Have you ever witnessed a race crime? If so, how was it dealt with?

- Why do you think that some people treat others of a different skin colour differently?

- Do you think there is a need to improve race relations:
  a) in your school?   b) in your local community?

WORK

1   **a** In your own words, explain what is meant by the Race Relations Act of 1976.

   b How did the Act change after 2000?

2   **a** Who was Stephen Lawrence?

   b How did his murder change British law?

   c Look at **Source C**. Why do you think the *Daily Mail* printed this article?

3   Look at **Source J**.

   a In what ways did the BNP get 'what they wanted'?

   b Why do you think the BNP has gained support in northern towns like Oldham and Burnley?

4   Below is a list of possible ways to improve race relations in Britain. Note down the advantages and disadvantages of each possible course of action:

   i)   stop all immigration.

   ii) send all people from an ethnic minority background back to their country from which their relatives/ancestors came from.

   iii) introduce harsher punishments for anyone found guilty of racist behaviour.

   iv) provide more education about race relations, race crime and so on.

   v)   provide money for more joint activities for the youth of different communities.

   vi) spend more money on facilities and improve living conditions in certain areas (so that people living there don't think that their lifestyle is made worse by ethnic minorities who have moved into the area).

   vii) make changes to the police force and encourage them to be more sensitive.

Case study: 'Let him have it!'

AIMS

Make sure you can:
- understand why the case of Derek Bentley caused such uproar in the 1950s;
- offer an opinion on the main arguments for and against the death penalty.

On Sunday 2 November 1952, in Croydon, Surrey, Derek Bentley (aged 19) and his friend Christopher Craig (aged 16) went out to commit a burglary. Both were armed – Bentley carried a knife and a **knuckle-duster** whilst Craig carried a knife and a gun.

As they climbed onto the roof of a warehouse, a little girl who lived opposite spotted them and her mother phoned the police. When the police arrived, Bentley was quickly detained but Craig tried to shoot his way out of trouble. At some time during the shoot out, Bentley is alleged to have shouted 'Let him have it Chris' to his friend. One policeman, PC Sidney Miles, was shot through the head and died almost instantly. Craig eventually ran out of bullets and jumped off the roof in an attempt to escape. He broke his back when he landed on a greenhouse ten metres below the warehouse roof.

Both Craig and Bentley were charged with the murder of PC Miles. But should Bentley have been charged with murder at all? The debate surrounding the case, and the consequences of it, raged for years and years. It raised a familiar old question – does Britain need capital punishment?

Source A ▶ Derek Bentley.

Both men went on trial in December 1952. Sixteen-year-old Craig was quickly found guilty and was sentenced to life imprisonment. He escaped a 'death by hanging' sentence due to the fact that he was only 16 and under the law, no one under 18 could be hanged. Derek Bentley though, was 19.

In Bentley's trial, the prosecution's main claim was that Bentley had shouted 'Let him have it Chris' to the killer. The prosecution took the phrase to mean that Bentley wanted Craig to shoot at the policeman and 'Let him have it'. There wasn't any definite proof he'd ever said this and even if he had, he could have simply meant for his friend to hand over the gun to the police.

After 75 minutes, the jury returned their verdict on Bentley – he too was found guilty of murder (the law states that if two or more people commit a crime, they can be held equally responsible for the outcome).

Despite the jury's recommendation for mercy (50% of all death sentences in the 1950s were reduced to life in prison) and the fact that Bentley had a mental age of 11, the plans for his execution still went ahead.

Immediately, there was a huge campaign against the execution. Campaigners argued that a man with a mental age of 11 should not face the death penalty ... *and* it wasn't actually Bentley who shot the policeman! Across Britain, arguments for and against the death penalty were voiced in newspapers, magazines, on the radio, in pubs and in people's front rooms.

Source B ▾ *A photograph of Christopher Craig, pictured in his football kit.*

Bentley's appeal against his conviction was turned down by the Court of Appeal on 13 January 1953, and he was hanged two weeks later on 28 January.

So what are the main arguments for and against capital punishment?

The main arguments supporting the death penalty

'It's too expensive to keep murderers in jail for the rest of their lives.'

'A life for a life, that's how I see it. Murderers give up their right to life when they take someone else's.'

'The death penalty is a message to those who might consider murder - our society will not tolerate you!'

'Reformers say that mistakes may happen and innocent people might be killed - but we have an intricate system of appeal so there are safeguards against that sort of thing. Mistakes hardly ever happen.'

'There aren't many executions every year anyway - and they're all cold-blooded vicious murderers. Why should we want to keep these people alive anyway?'

The main arguments against the death penalty

'Mistakes <u>do</u> happen - and you can't reverse the death penalty.'

'The death penalty doesn't deter murderers. We had a death penalty for centuries and murders still happened. Why keep the death penalty when it clearly doesn't work?'

'It's barbaric - we live in a civilised society don't we? Not one that kills its prisoners!'

'Life imprisonment is an adequate punishment - at least they are removed from society.'

'The death penalty is hardly used anyway. Between 1900 and 1954, there were over 7000 murder convictions. Of these people, 1210 received the death sentence - but only 632 were carried out.'

Source C ▾ Let him have it!

Let him Dangle   by Elvis Costello

"Bentley said to Craig 'let him have it Chris'
          They still don't know today just what he meant by this
Craig fired the pistol, but was too young to swing
          So the police took Bentley and the very next thing
Let him dangle
          Let him dangle

          Bentley had surrendered, he was under arrest,
                    When he gave Chris Craig that fatal request
          Craig shot Sidney Miles, he took Bentley's word
                    The prosecution claimed as they charged them with murder
          Let him dangle
                    Let him dangle

Source D ▾ A crowd gather outside Wandsworth Prison to learn about the execution of Derek Bentley.

The story of Bentley and Craig has generated several books, a film, hundreds of magazine articles and news items and even some songs (see **Source C**). In November 1997, after a long campaign to clear his name of murder, Bentley's case was referred to the Court of Appeal. After re-examining the evidence, the verdict of 'guilty' was quashed. After 46 years, Derek Bentley was proclaimed an innocent man.

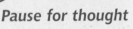

Pause for thought

According to Bentley's hangman, what was public opinion like in Britain with regard to Bentley's execution?

Source E ▼ *Bentley's hangman, Albert Pierrepoint, writing about the atmosphere in the country in the lead up to his execution.*

"The jury, who found both lads guilty of murder, added a recommendation of mercy for Bentley ... a storm of public feeling blew up. It increased as Bentley's last days slipped by. His appeal was dismissed and protest marches by crowds, pleas in Parliament, went all unheeded by the authorities.

The storm was going on when I received the long grey envelope asking me to attend at Wandsworth Prison to hang Bentley. As I peered from the upper windows of the No 77 bus which took me to Wandsworth the day before the execution, I saw newspaper placards along every street proclaiming: 'MPs fight to save Bentley'.

So even 16 hours before the execution was due, there was still doubt it would take place...

But the morning papers carried headlines saying only that there was to be 'no reprieve for Bentley' and I knew I would have my job to do."

Fact *Last two!*

The last two men to be hanged in the UK were executed at exactly the same time in different places. Peter Anthony Allen and John Robson Walby were hanged on 13 August 1964 for the murder of John Alan West.

Source F ▾ An article by Duncan Campbell on the Bentley case, written in 1997.

"The bottle of Moet & Chandon champagne that had been sitting in a south London cupboard for 40 years was finally opened yesterday to celebrate the quashing of Derek Bentley's conviction for the murder of PC Sidney Miles.

Since William Bentley bought the bottle in 1958 in expectation of toasting his son's pardon, the family has experienced many raised and dashed hopes. In the Court of Appeal yesterday, the long crusade reached its conclusion.

The Lord Chief Justice, Lord Bingham, sitting with Lord Justice Kennedy and Mr Justice Collins, quashed the conviction in a 52-page judgement that secretly criticised his predecessor Lord Goddard, ruled that the conviction had been unsafe because of the judge's intemperate summing-up and expressed regret that the mistrial had not been spotted soon enough to save Bentley.

Maria Dingwall-Bentley, who has led the campaign to clear her uncle's name since her mother, Iris Bentley, died of cancer last year, said she was elated by the result but sad that her mother was not alive to see it.

'I'm absolutely thrilled,' she said as she popped the cork and declared the champagne much better than expected. 'The British justice system has had a death on its hands for all those years.'"

WISE UP WORD
• knuckle-duster

WORK

1 a In the Bentley murder trial, why was there confusion over the phrase 'Let him have it!'?
 b Christopher Craig murdered PC Miles. So why was Bentley on trial for murder at all?
 c Why do you think there was a campaign against Bentley's execution?

2 The death penalty was abolished in 1965 ... after much national debate.
 a Why do you think some people wanted to keep the death penalty?
 b Why do you think others wanted to get rid of it?
 c What is your opinion?
 • Was the government of 1965 right to abolish the death penalty?
 • Should they have abolished it for a trial period?
 • Should it be reintroduced?

Write an answer, of no more than 250 words, answering the question, 'Does Britain need capital punishment?'

SUMMARY

• The police and detective forces use the latest technological advances to catch crooks. Criminals use the latest technology too. The two-court system – Magistrate and Crown Courts – try all cases. The Crown (Royal) Court uses juries to try serious cases whilst the Magistrates' Court, using three magistrates, tries less serious ones.

• Recorded crime increased rapidly in the latter half of the twentieth century. However, there were a lot more crimes as a result of new technology (car and computer crime for example) and it was easier than ever before to report crime (using telephones and so on). In 2000, it was reported that the fear of violent crime had trebled since 1990!

• Britain's prison population is amongst the highest in Europe. More prisons have been built and the main focus is still on punishment and reform.

Crime and punishment: a summary

In each period of history covered in this book, theft has been the most common crime. And despite what some newspapers would have us believe, violent crime – assault, murder and rape for example – is at its lowest levels for centuries. But, as you know, crime is punished very differently in different periods in history. In fact, what is seen as a crime depends very much on the era in which the crime has taken place. Policing too, and the trials that decide on a person's guilt, have changed dramatically over the years.

This double page then aims to summarise crime, punishment, policing and trials in each of the periods of history covered in this book. Study each source very carefully.

Source A ▾ *Percentage of all crime attributed to petty theft (theft of clothing, food, small amounts of money and so on).*

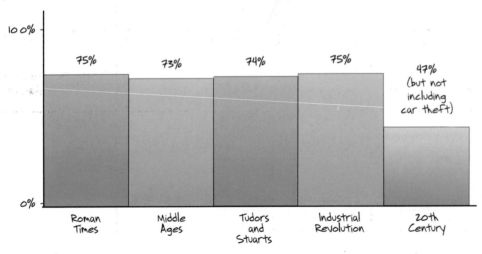

Source B ▸ *Violent crime as a percentage of total crime.*

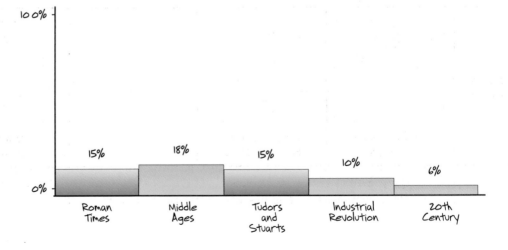

Source C ▾ *Types of punishment from Roman times to the Modern World.*

	Roman Times	Middle Ages	Tudors and Stuarts	Industrial Britain	20th Century Britain
Custody	Slavery	Prison		Hard labour	Prisons fuller than ever/probation and 'tagging' used
				DORSET ANY PERSON WILFULLY INJURING ANY PART OF THIS COUNTY BRIDGE WILL BE GUILTY OF FELONY AND UPON CONVICTION LIABLE TO BE TRANSPORTED FOR LIFE BY THE COURT — Transportation — Ended in 1868	
Fines	Repayment to victim	Wergilds to victim	Fine to victim and King		Fines still common form of punishment
Humiliation	Public beatings	Stocks and pillory			
Capital punishment	Crucifixion/fight to death	Public hanging/ burnt at stake		Hanging in private	Death penalty abolished in 1965
	500BC-AD400	400-1500	1500-1750	1750-1900	1900-2000

Speech bubbles: "Goodness, I'm bored!", "I feel more like a hamster every day!"

Source D ▾ *Trials through the ages.*

	Roman Times	Middle Ages	Tudors and Stuarts	Industrial Britain	20th Century Britain
Judges and juries	Judge and jury use evidence	Judge and jury use evidence and knowledge of offender		Judge and jury use evidence	
Trial	Jury trial	Jury trial and trial by ordeal	Jury trial and defence/prosecution lawyers		
	500BC-AD400	400-1500	1500-1750	1750-1900	1900-2000

<u>Source E</u> ▾ *Policing.*

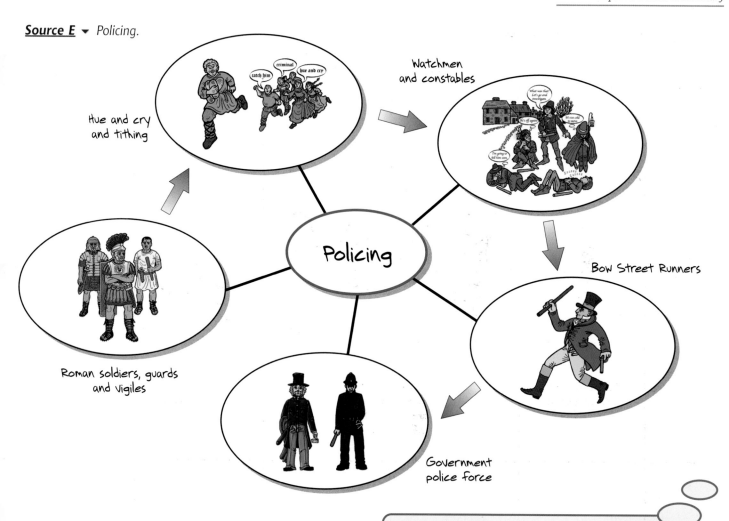

Hue and cry and tithing

Watchmen and constables

Roman soldiers, guards and vigiles

Policing

Bow Street Runners

Government police force

Pause for thought

How do today's Magistrates' Court and Crown Court differ? Which has a jury? Who makes up these juries? If only one has a jury, what does the other type of court use?

WORK

1 **a** What is the most common type of crime in all periods studied in this book?

   b Can you think of reasons why this crime has remained the most common?

2 Look at **Source B**.

   According to this chart, are newspaper articles which claim we live in the 'most violent period ever' correct? Give reasons for your answer.

3 Look at **Source C**.

   a Choose three punishments from the chart which are no longer used today. Explain why each is no longer used.

   b Look at the following list of reasons why people are punished:

   i) to deter the criminals themselves from committing other crimes

   ii) to change the criminals so they feel that crime doesn't pay

   iii) to compensate the victim in some way

   iv) to protect society

   v) to warn others away from a life of crime.

   Match a punishment from the chart to each of the five reasons.

4 Look at **Source D**.

   Why do you think judges and juries have consistently been used to try offenders throughout the periods studied in this book?

5 Look at **Source E**.

   a In your own words, explain how policing has changed since Roman times.

   b In your opinion, when was the period of greatest change in policing? Give reasons for your opinion.

Have you been learning?

TASK 1: ODD TWO OUT

Here are eight sentences. Each sentence has two errors. One is a spelling mistake; the other is a factual error. When you have spotted the mistakes, write the sentence out correctly.

a Elizabeth Fry was one of several reformers who spent there time trying to improve the lives of prisoners and conditions in prisons. Her work was so valued that in 2002, she was chosen to appear on Britain's new £10 note.

b Britain's first proffessional police force was set up by Robert Peel in London in 1827.

c In the 1820s, there were over 200 capitol crimes. These were crimes that could lead to a prisoner facing execution if convicted. The criminal justice system at this time was known as 'the bleeding code'.

d One of Britain's most infamous cereal killers, Jack the Ripper, was never caught. Despite many witness sightings and several good suspects, he avoided capture and the murder of several prostitutes in the 1980s remains unsolved.

e The Luddites were a violent protest group who smashed up mashines because it had taken away their farm labouring jobs.

f Captain Swing was the imaginary leader of a group of protesters who smashed up factorys in London in the 1830s.

g The Charterists demanded changes to the voting laws, including votes for everyone over the age of 21.

h The Tolpuddle Marters were transported to America for swearing a secret oath on the Bible when they met to discuss their farm wages in 1833. The whole episode caused a huge outcry and the seven men returned to Britain in 1836.

TASK 2: EXECUTION TIME

Source A ▾ Execution at Tyburn.

Source B ▾ A description of the execution.

'On the day of execution, the condemned prisoners are tied two together and placed on carts with their backs to the horses' tails. These carts are guarded and surrounded by constables and other police officers on horseback, armed with a sort of pike.'

Tyburn is reached, and here stands the gibbet. One often sees criminals going to their death perfectly unconcerned; others fill themselves full of liquor. When all the prisoners arrive, they are made to mount on a very wide cart made for the purpose; a cord is passed round their necks and the end fastened to the gibbet. The chaplain who accompanies the condemned men is also on the cart; he makes them pray and sing a few verses of the Psalms.

The relatives are permitted to mount the cart and take farewell. When the time is up, the chaplain and the relations get off the cart, which slips from under the condemned men's feet. In this way, they remain all hanging together.

You often see friends and relations tugging at the hanging man's feet so that they should die quicker. The bodies and clothes of the dead belong to the executioner; relatives must, if they wish for them, buy them from him. Unclaimed bodies are sold to surgeons to be dissected. You see most amusing scenes between the people who do not like the bodies to be cut up and the messengers whom the surgeons have sent for the bodies; blows are given and returned before they can be got away.'

1 Look at **Source A**. Write down the numbers 1–6 in your book and next to each number, try to explain what is going on in the scene.

2 Look at **Source B**.
   a Why do you think there were a lot of constables and guards at these executions?
   b Why do you think some prisoners got very drunk?
   c Why do you think the hanging gibbet was so big?
   d Why did some of the relatives of the prisoners pull on their feet after they had been hanged?
   e What happened to some of the unclaimed bodies?

TASK 3: ODD ONE OUT

Below are ten groups of words. Work out which is the odd one out in each and say why.

a fine • whipping • stocks • pillory
b hot iron • ordeal • bread • cold water
c rack • boot • press • Tower
d Royal • Manor • village • church
e watchmen • constables • Justices of the Peace • smuggler
f sturdy beggar • bristler • clapper dudgeon • angler
g Wat Tyler • Robert Aske • Guy Fawkes • Robert Kett
h Peelers • Bobbies • blue devils • Sir Robert Peel
i transportation • forging bank notes • shooting rabbits • treason
j Mary Ann Nichols • Annie Chapman • Mary Kelly • George Lusk

TASK 4: SUMMARY

Draw a table like the one below and use your knowledge of crime and punishment in Medieval England and Tudor and Stuart England to complete it. The policing box has been started for you.

	BRITAIN IN 1500–1750	BRITAIN IN 1750–1900	IN YOUR OPINION, DID THINGS CHANGE OR STAY THE SAME?
LAWS			
POLICING	No police force; tithing and hue and cry used. Leading villagers were appointed as constables and watchmen.	A professional police force replaced the old system of unpaid constables and watchmen.	
TRIALS			
PUNISHMENTS			

TASK 5: QUESTION TIME

Look at these genuine GCSE questions carefully. Why not try to complete them as a revision exercise? In brackets after each question, you will find the pages of this book where there is information that might refresh your memory.

• The Rebecca Riots and the suffragettes are both examples of popular protests. Briefly explain the aims of either the Rebecca rioters or the suffragettes.
(pages 105, 112–113)

• Compare the ways in which the Kett rebels and the General Strikers challenged the authorities. How similar were they? Explain your answer.
(pages 42–43, 114–115)

Glossary

abolish   To bring to an end/to do away with. For example, the death penalty.

alibi   Pleas of being somewhere else when a crime was committed.

ancient world   The period in history, starting about 5000 years ago, when civilizations such as the Egyptians, the Greeks and then the Romans dominated.

approver   A person, found guilty of a crime, who is declared innocent if they can find ten other people who have committed crimes.

benefit of the clergy   A claim, meaning you have the right to go on a trial in a Church Court.

blood feud   The legal right of a murder victim's family to hunt down and kill the murderer in revenge.

Bloody Code   The name given to the period between 1700 and 1800 when harsh laws with tough punishments were introduced.

borstals   Special new 'schools', set up in 1899, which were used to encourage young offenders to 'change for the better'.

broadsheet   An early type of newspaper.

canting   A secretive language used by sturdy beggars in Tudor England.

capital offence   A crime that carries the death penalty as a punishment.

Chartists   A group who demanded changes to the voting system between 1837 and 1848. They were called Chartists after their six-point charter, or list of demands.

Church Court   A special court that tried only members of the clergy or people connected to the Church.

Conscientious Objectors   A person who refuses to join the armed forces.

constable   Men from every village who were appointed to uphold law and order. They did it in their own time and didn't get paid.

crucifixion   An ancient punishment involving putting someone to death by nailing them to a cross.

decimation   The murder of every tenth person in a group.

Digest of Roman Law   A book of Roman laws, written in about 500AD.

exile   Banishment from one's home or country.

folk moots   An open air trial that took place in Saxon times.

Forest Laws   Unpopular laws introduced by William the Conqueror, which aimed to protect his forests.

general strike   A strike by people from different industries.

highway robbery   Robbing a traveller or a stage coach that is making the journey between towns.

House of Correction   A type of prison where convicted criminals were sent.

hue and cry   A noisy group of villagers who chased suspected criminals.

hulks   Old warships used as prisons.

import duties   Taxes on any goods coming into a country.

Justice of the Peace   A government official who tried to keep law and order in towns.

knuckle-duster   A piece of metal that fits over fingers, used to hit someone.

libel   A false statement that is published and which damages somebody's reputation.

Luddites   A group of protesters who smashed up factory equipment.

magistrate   A local official who acts as a judge.

Manor Court A court for less serious crimes that met several times a year in the local lord's manor house. Punishment was usually a fine.

modus operandi Method of killing someone.

Normans The ruling group in England between 1066 and about 1160.

oath-helper A type of witness prepared to swear on a cross that a person is innocent.

outlaw A person who is being hunted for his crimes but has so far evaded capture.

phosphorus A wax that ignites in the air; used to make matches.

pillory
A wooden frame with holes for head and hands.

reformatory schools Tough schools that aimed to change young criminals so they would no longer commit crimes.

Roman Empire The area of land dominated by the Romans between 500BC and 400AD.

Royal Court Courts that dealt with serious crimes and met in the name of the king. Sometimes known as a Shire Court.

sanctuary A safe place, such as a church. Once a person claimed sanctuary, they could not be removed by force.

separate system A type of prison punishment in the 1800s where prisoners were kept completely separate from each other.

Shire Court   A court for more serious crimes that met a few times a year in the county town.

silent system   A type of prison punishment in the 1800s where prisoners were kept in complete silence.

stocks   A punishment device made of a wooden frame, with holes for the feet.

sturdy beggar   A criminal who used clever tricks to get money.

ticket of leave   A piece of paper that gave a transported prisoner permission to go back to Britain.

tithing   Groups of ten men who were responsible for each other's behaviour. If a member of a tithing broke the law, the others had to catch him and pay his fine.

trade union   An organisation of workers to protect their interests.

transportation   A punishment, meaning to be sent away (transported) to another country for a set period of time.

trial by ordeal   A medieval way of finding out if a person was guilty or not.

Twelve Tables   Some of the first written Roman laws, circa 450BC.

vagabonds   Poor people who wandered the streets in Tudor England looking for food and shelter.

vigiles   Officials who patrolled the streets of Rome at night, trying to prevent crime.

watch   Men who patrolled the streets during the night, trying to prevent crime.

wergild   A form of compensation paid to the victims of crime in Saxon times.

Index